Toward a Mankind School:
An Adventure in Humanistic Education

TOWARD A MANKIND SCHOOL:
AN ADVENTURE IN HUMANISTIC EDUCATION

John I. Goodlad
M. Frances Klein
Jerrold M. Novotney
Kenneth A. Tye

and Associates:

Margaret J. Brown
Edith B. Buchanan
Margaret J. Burke
Lillian K. Drag
Judith S. Golub
Gerhard Hirschfeld
Roxie Lee
Kent Lewis
Donald A. Myers
Douglas O. Russell

McGRAW-HILL BOOK COMPANY

New York   St. Louis   San Francisco   Düsseldorf   London
Mexico   Sydney   Toronto

Library of Congress Cataloging in Publication Data
Main entry under title:

Toward a mankind school.

Bibliography: p.
1. Education, Humanistic. 2. Interpersonal relations. I. Goodlad, John I.
LC1021.T68   370.11'2   74-14758
ISBN 0-07-023624-0

Acknowledgments for permission to use excerpts from copyrighted material include:

Teilhard de Chardin, *The Phenomenon of Man.* Copyright 1961 by Teilhard de Chardin. Used by permission of Harper & Row.

Erik H. Erikson, *Childhood and Society.* Copyright 1963 by W. W. Norton and Company, Inc.

John I. Goodlad, "Some Propositions in Search of Schools." Copyright 1962 by the National Association of Elementary School Principals.

Barbara Leondar, "The Counterschool Approach." Copyright 1971 by the American Labor Conference on International Affairs, Inc.

G. Lesser, *Psychology and the Educational Process.* Copyright 1971 by Scott, Foresman and Company. Used by permission of Scott, Foresman and Company.

Louis J. Rubin, *Facts and Feelings in the Classroom.* Copyright 1973 by Louis J. Rubin. Used by permission of Walker and Company, Inc.

Robert Ulich, *Education and the Idea of Mankind.* Copyright 1964 by Robert Ulich. Used by permission of Harcourt Brace Jovanovich.

Contents

Introduction

More and more persons, more and more governments, more and more peoples are becoming aware of the fact that no man is an island unto himself, no nation governs itself for long unmindful of other nations, and no people is unaffected by the actions of other peoples. The individual, the nation, or the people pursuing a mindless, self-indulgent course offends the sensibilities, endangers the health, or threatens the lives of others. Today, as never before, our problems must be approached from a mankind perspective and with mankind solutions. But, as yet, we have neither the perspective nor the solutions.

The fact that we have neither should not deter us from seeking them. The need is urgent and the time is short. Starvation taking the lives of thousands in one country; horrible plagues crossing national boundaries to cut down men, women, and children; a belt of pollution encircling the globe; hostile eruptions capable of engulfing the whole world in war—these and other problems of similar magnitude reveal the absence of any mechanisms capable of coping with them. We play games of protocol like games of chess, as though there will be winners and losers even when the stakes are mankind itself.

Most of us rouse ourselves from our reveries occasionally, as though from troubled sleep, long enough to become dimly aware that all of this is true, that man may very well be on a course toward destruction. Usually, however, we soon return to these reveries, preoccupied with narcissistic interests and pursuits. Even if our awareness of mankind persists, we are soon overcome with a feeling of ennui, hopelessness, or impotence. The problems are of such gravity and magnitude that they defy comprehension, let alone solutions to which we can contribute significantly as individuals. We return to our reveries.

Like most others, I too find refuge in my reveries. Except for occasional pangs of conscience, more sharply excruciating at some periods of life than at others, I adjusted fairly comfortably to my myopia. In the late 1950s, however, I received a letter that stirred me and led me to paths I had not followed before. It came at one of those periods when a usually dormant mankind conscience was pricking more than usual. The letter was from Gerhard Hirschfeld, Executive Director of the Council for the Study of Mankind, Inc., inviting me to write a chapter for a book, *Education and the Idea of Mankind,* to be edited by Robert Ulich.

Preparing for and writing that chapter, together with subsequent years of association with the Council, have brought a somewhat heightened awareness of mankind and the urgency of our mankind problems. They have brought, also, many troublesome questions about how one develops a mankind perspective, participates productively in mankind processes and activities, and contributes to mankind solutions. A person is not born with a mankind awareness; he develops it or learns it. Therefore, one cannot contemplate mankind for long without contemplating education, too. It appears self-evident that the advancement of mankind and education go hand in hand.

But such a conclusion only reveals still other troublesome questions. What kind of education advances the mankind idea and mankind behavior? What should be the content, the method, the setting? Are some periods of life more propitious than others for the learning desired? Are there certain sensitive periods in human development that present teachable moments? These are age-old educational problems. The answers are, at best, tentative and temporary, whatever the realm of human experience under consideration for educational purposes. But the ground remains virgin, the soil scarcely touched, when we come to consider education for mankind. We must begin to till this potentially productive soil.

With this end in view, I presented to the Board of Directors of the Council for the Study of Mankind a proposal for a project that would seek to explore the idea of mankind with children. Subsequently, the Ford Foundation provided a grant to support the project under the joint auspices of the Council and Educational Inquiry, Inc., a nonprofit educational research organization. The first step was to extract and collate relevant concepts and ideas about mankind from the works of the Council. The second was to prepare a segment of curriculum for children. The third was to teach from a mankind perspective both a group of elementary school children and a parallel group of teachers. All three steps proved to be extraordinarily difficult, exceeding in magnitude even our own considerable trepidations about them.

Four of us who attempted the first step—Donald A. Myers, Jerrold M. Novotney, Kenneth A. Tye, and myself—owe to the fifth, M. Frances Klein, an enormous debt of gratitude. She went through the various documents of the Council, searching for ideas which might be meaningful to children; she brought to our attention what should be read by all of us in common; she saw to it that we met with reasonable frequency and with a predetermined agenda, and she kept us to our writing schedules.[1] Further, after the first year, Frances Klein worked closely with the teachers who developed the curriculum for children. Finally, she and Jerrold M. Novotney conducted the workshop for teachers, the concluding portion of the third step to which we had committed ourselves.

The first inclination of all of us associated with this report is to apologize

1. In the midst of our deliberations, Donald Myers accepted an academic appointment elsewhere. He contributed significantly to our initial conception of mankind schooling and, for the first year, worked with several teachers from the University Elementary School, UCLA, who prepared and taught the curriculum for children.

to the Council for the Study of Mankind for slighting many ideas, distorting others, and leaving out many significant ones, perhaps the most significant; and to the reader for the incompleteness, tentativeness, and fuzziness of our concepts. But there is no point in doing so. After perusing what follows, the reader will, no doubt, share in some of the feelings of inadequacy we have experienced from the beginning. Also, the Council has spoken eloquently for itself; some of its major publications are cited on subsequent pages.[2] Only some of its deliberations and statements, however, are appropriate in seeking to educate children.

This book is divided into three parts. Chapters 1 through 4 report on the first step: identifying some of the basic ideas and their possible meaning for education and schooling. Chapters 5 and 6 report on the second step: translating these ideas into a curriculum and pedagogical procedures and conducting an experimental summer program for children at the University Elementary School, UCLA. Chapter 7 contains our reflections on the project and its implications for the future.

Chapter 1 is the only chapter dealing with mankind as such: the issues and their urgency, the mankind perspective, and the linkage between education and the mankind idea. Chapters 2 through 4 are concerned with schooling— the setting or environment conducive to educating for mankind, the interpersonal relationships that should prevail, and the subject matter appropriate to schooling with a mankind perspective.

Chapters 5 and 6 are of a different order. Here, we endeavor to report on our experiences with children and teachers. Those of us who began the first step of the project had met from time to time for a year before the work involved in actually creating a curriculum was begun. Then we were successful in attracting the interest of several widely experienced members of the faculty of the University Elementary School, UCLA: Margaret Brown, Edith Buchanan, Douglas Russell, Roxie Lee, and Kent Lewis. They took on the task of finding ways to bring mankind awareness and processes into the lives of children. Although there was general agreement that young children, probably between the ages of three and six, presented us with unique opportunities for what we had in mind, we perceived pedagogical difficulties arising primarily out of our inability to design appropriate activities. We decided, therefore, to seek entry during the upper elementary school years, between the ages of approximately nine and twelve.

Planning how, specifically, to enter the lives of preadolescent children was exceedingly difficult. There were many false starts and even more compromises. Some ideas were abandoned simply because financial resources were not adequate or because replication by others would be difficult. For

2. Two recent ones are W. Warren Wagar (ed.), *History and the Idea of Mankind,* The University of New Mexico Press, Albuquerque, 1971, and Gerhard Hirschfeld, *The People,* Aldine Publishing Company, Chicago, 1973.

example, we thought it highly desirable that the participating children become involved, for some weeks, in the daily activities of a contrasting culture, but this idea presented logistical difficulties that could not be overcome within our financial and time constraints. The planning activities are described in Chapter 5.

As stated earlier, the culminating activity of the entire project was a summer program for children and a parallel institute for teachers. In this volume we concentrate on discussing the program for children. The Appendix presents a course outline and description of the teacher workshop. We hold no special brief for the activities planned and conducted. In general, they were a reflection of the ideas presented in Chapters 1 through 4. Undoubtedly, other activities would have served as well or better. The report presented here is designed to encourage others, not to present *the way* to create increased awareness of mankind.

We were fortunate in securing the services of Margaret J. Burke, who observed the children and teachers at work over the six-week period of the summer program. Chapter 6 is based on her report. Throughout the life of the project, a period of almost three years, Lillian K. Drag participated in our discussions and assisted us in securing appropriate readings. The report which follows concludes with an annotated bibliography which she prepared. A final editing and rewriting to prepare the manuscript for publication was the responsibility of Judith S. Golub. In addition, Carmen M. Culver provided valuable editorial suggestions at various stages.

The authors and associate authors of this volume generously gave their time and energy to the project without compensation. All are very busy people. All of us took great inspiration from another of the associate authors—Gerhard Hirschfeld. Hirschfeld has devoted most of his life and limited financial resources to the idea and the cause of mankind. Mankind and the Council for the Study of Mankind, Inc., which he founded, have been his vocation and his avocation. He was the spark that ignited us and has been our continuing inspiration. This project would not have commenced, let alone continued, without him.

I conclude by expressing appreciation to the Council for the Study of Mankind for encouragement, to the Ford Foundation for financial support and an accompanying belief in the worth of the enterprise, and to all those who contributed to the project throughout its existence. Regarding this last group, I thank Madeline Hunter, principal of the University Elementary School, for her help in planning the summer activities for children and teachers; Theodore Brameld, Elliot Eisner, Sol Tax, Egbert de Vries, and Thomas LaBelle for consultation; and the children and teachers who joined us for the summer activities.

We are too close to these culminating activities to evaluate them in proper perspective. However, the children appeared not to have any difficulty with the mankind perspective. The teachers, like almost everyone else coming to the mankind idea, often were frustrated with the vagueness of concepts and the fuzziness of terms. Nonetheless, they appeared to develop a "feel" for mankind and a sense of urgency regarding mankind problems. We trust that they will make a beginning with children, just as we have taken, we hope, a step toward a mankind school.

Royalties received from this publication will be devoted exclusively to our continuing work on education for mankind.

John I. Goodlad

Chapter 1
Education for Mankind

At some time or other in history, most of the major regions of the earth have had their spokesmen for some vision of oneness or unity among inhabitants of the known world. The idea of mankind is not new.

In India, Buddhism spoke to the impermanence of the world and its earthbound restraints, offering to all both the promise and the ultimate experience of transcending these. Even before the beginnings of Buddhism in the sixth century B.C., however, the idea of human unity was deeply embedded in Indian thought, albeit within a stratified or caste system of diversity. Buddhist rejection of this Brahmanic order of the world deeply influenced general ideas about mankind.

China had Confucianism, taking as its ultimate aim the achievement of universal harmony in a global commonwealth. It is noteworthy that Confucius lived in troubled times of warring states with separate traditions and ideologies, and yet it was on Confucian principles of interstate order that China survived to modern times.

Jewish universalism espouses a concept of monotheism in which God and the world he created are each one. The concept of mankind was embedded also in the very beginnings of Islamic thought, ultimately finding expression in the idea that mankind becomes one as man sees himself in the true image of God. Muhammad spoke to all men, not to a select few. And the Greek philosophers and early Christian church addressed themselves frequently to the idea of human unity.

We need not go back so far in history, however, because we readily find concepts of transcendental spiritual unity or human oneness in modern thinkers and philosophers such as Gandhi, Marx, Tillich, and de Chardin. Through all of man's troubled history, the idea of mankind has been present, though it has too often been ignored. It can be no longer, for time is running out. Our task is to create an orderly world, a proper environment for the whole of mankind. Whether the City of Man[1] can be created before a global holocaust destroys the historical promise and, some predict, mankind itself is a race of desperate significance.

The Mankind Imperative

Mankind is the only framework within which solutions for the vast problems of human society can be found. No single nation or small group of nations can abolish war. No single industry or group of industries can deal effectively with the maldistribution of world productivity. No public or private agency can deal with starvation, population growth, pollution, health and medical care, the effective growth and utilization of automation, or a host of other global problems. Only the concerted efforts and resources of all of mankind have the potential to embrace the problems, derive solutions, and exercise the authority to implement these solutions.

But it is not easy to acknowledge and obey this mankind imperative. As we look at our response to opportunities to concern ourselves with mankind, we are inclined to believe that Teilhard de Chardin was optimistic in his conclusion that "no-one can' escape being haunted or even dominated by the idea of mankind."[2] We are not dominated by the idea of mankind in allowing the once slow but now full-throttle rape of the earth's resources and pollution of the air and water. Nor have we yet seized the opportunity being presented to concern ourselves with mankind in our exploration of the poles, the desert, the ocean bed, and outer space. Even highly visible and immediately threatening problems such as nuclear war, immorality, drug addiction, population growth, starvation, and loss of identity have not awakened a mankind conscience or evoked a mankind response. Neither the problems nor the opportunities will present themselves much longer. The time has come to make a personal commitment to mankind as a down payment on the mankind behavior our times demand or abandon hope of attaining the controls essential to survival. The reality of our age is both this simple and this complex.

Why not take the simple step and commit ourselves to mankind? Any attempt to answer this question reveals its inherent complexity.

For one thing, the idea of mankind as an indivisible entity is hardly known. "However far science pushes its discovery of the 'essential' fire and however capable it becomes of remodeling and perfecting the human element, it will always find itself in the end facing the same problem—how to give to each and every element its final value by grouping them in the unity of an organized whole."[3] For another, a concern with mankind is not like a job or an enterprise where one consigns oneself to certain duties. One can only commit oneself to a determination to strive for attainment of that which in one's opinion is likely to advance the cause of mankind.

Even such a basic commitment is difficult. We are brought up in partisan identifications and thought patterns. Encouraged to think primarily as Americans or Chinese, Christians or Jews, Buddhists or Muslims, communists or capitalists, black or brown or white or yellow, we interpret the beliefs and aspirations of other people in the light of our indoctrination. Each of us is tied to long-established values, loyalties, traditions, languages, and relationships. To expect people to loosen these ties sufficiently to make room for the awareness of mankind and to recognize the mankind imperative is expecting a great deal. And so, traveling the mankind road, whatever its nature and course, demands determination and painful reorientation. The motivation is compelling. There probably is nothing wrong with our world, convulsed and troubled though it is, that concerted action cannot cure if the motivation is the welfare of mankind and if a significant portion of mankind participates guided by a mankind perspective.

A Mankind Perspective

Mankind is the totality of man and his society, embracing in a vast sweep all of his learning, institutions, aspirations and fears, morality and immorality, faith and cynicism, the past and the present. Each person born into this society inherits a slice of the whole. But the individual and mankind are not identical, any more than the grain of sand and the beach are identical.

Mankind is universal. One can no better understand mankind from simply understanding oneself than one can understand a symphony from the twelve notes of the scale or a chemical compound from its atoms. One must transcend self, friends, and neighbors in the endless struggle to become aware of and to understand mankind as a unifying concept—all people and their institutions, all nations and religions, all cultures and civilizations, past and present, and in anticipation of their future. Nothing short of the reality of the human society as a single whole can be accepted as the concept of mankind.

This necessary wholeness is elusive, defying our efforts to define, describe, or circumscribe it in any precise way. Perhaps, at best, one simply intuits it. But the concept or idea of mankind can and must provide a perspective from which to view the specifics. Ulich sums up both the conceptual difficulty and the necessary perspective:

> Even when we try to extend the span of our interest as far as possible, the whole is beyond our grasp; it exists only in our vision, or intuition. Yet, without a picture of the whole, we cannot even comprehend the single. Behind and within every leaf we see whole nature, and it is the same with every person. And behind every person is also his society, his nation and its history, mankind, and finally the universe. It is good to remind ourselves from time to time of all this infinity in order to acquire this healthy relativism, which should prevent us from idolizing ourselves and our nation, our creeds, our truths, and our little knowledge.[4]

Mankind is more than just an idea or a concept, however. It is a reality; it exists. Whether or not its constituent elements are in disjuncture and to some degree sick and even decaying and dying is quite beside the point. By perceiving it as reality, we can begin to create the activities required to close the gap between the idealized concept and functioning reality.

Mankind, then, is also a process, operating as a global system of interacting people and societies in a world infused both by doubt, confusion, contradiction, and hostility and by strivings, hopes, and ideals. Subprocesses of man-to-man and nation-to-nation interactions promote or conserve fear, suspicion, hatred, oppression, love, kindness, support, nationalism, racism, war, harmony, acceptance, peace. Mankind as reality and process is enhanced or is diminished because of these subprocesses and their repercussions. A mankind perspective requires that we see the importance of all the components of these processes and recognize that even a simple and apparently unimportant action can have far-reaching consequences. The wastes a city dumps into a river can destroy the livelihood of fishermen many miles away.

Just as Pusey has suggested that God cannot be fully encompassed by our minds,[5] mankind in all its wholeness eludes us, too. Therefore, to mankind as a concept and a process must be added faith and commitment—commitment to things that are real because they are life itself.

The primary effort to attain awareness and understanding of mankind—a mankind perspective—should be directed initially to reorientation of the mind of the individual person. From the beginning, the goal becomes to acquire the intellectual tools for understanding mankind and commitment to and faith in the mankind idea. The process is not one of merely relating oneself to mankind. It is a process of self-transcending thought, commitment, and action. Phenix captures it, in part:

> ...the rationalist faith is that there is one standpoint—that of disciplined reason—which comprehends all the others, making it possible to escape the relativities of time and culture and the illusions of provincialism. This is the peculiar property of reason, that it enables man to achieve a degree of universality, to rise to some extent above the limitations of circumstance and history....In this

power of self-transcendence lies the justification for the concept of mankind and for an approach to education formed around that idea.[6]

We have only a dim understanding of the concept; most of the processes escape our grasp; the commitment is largely intuitive. When pressed for definition, description, and justification, we are tempted to say, "If I have to tell you, you will never understand." But we can study the mind's processes, even the subtleties of self-transcendence, and we can see all around us the effects of man's blunders and inhumanity to man. The mankind perspective is not a romantic one. It is a rational one, combining elusive qualities: "The first is the quality of faith, the second the quality of self-transcendence and the third the quality of vision—all three disciplined and purified by reason and self-criticism."[7]

The concept of rationality can be pushed even further by positing a necessary relationship among understanding, commitment, and action:

> The rational man not only is committed to the rich fruits of inquiry but also is prepared to act and, indeed, acts upon insight rendered compelling by commitment. He knows, as perhaps the most vital ingredient of his rationality, that only through action following understanding and commitment does man forge the links in the chains of his own humanity and of mankind's immortality. He senses his place in time and space and his individual responsibility to that place, time, and space.[8]

To many, the very rationality of the mankind perspective constitutes its weakness. "Man is not rational," they say. "He is not, has not been, and never will be rational. Man's irrationality cannot be resolved through rational processes." Or, as Jung has said, "The whole world wants peace and the whole world prepares for war....Mankind is powerless against mankind."[9] But still the analyst seeks, through his understanding of the mind and the individual, to have his patient acquire increased rationality and control over his own destiny. And so it must be with mankind. But there is little hope for the individual or mankind unless there is a collective shaping of the conditions impinging upon and guiding individual and group behavior. Education presents our major opportunity to provide this shaping.

Mankind and Education

If the mankind perspective is a rational one, involving understanding, commitment, and action, and if man must be reoriented, then it becomes clear that education has a significant role to play. We must make clear, however, that education is not enough. Education is the long-term answer to the mankind condition. Enlightened social engineering is the answer for the short term. Present and embryonic wars, pollution, and the population explosion cannot await long-term solutions. The future of mankind depends on global action now, even when we are not educated for it.

The need is so urgent that to talk about long-term solutions to our mankind dilemmas may be to talk about no solutions at all. Nonetheless, we are addressing ourselves in this volume to relatively long-term solutions (although the time is minuscule against the backdrop of our mankind history)—solutions pertaining to the education of children.

We must make clear, also, that education and schooling are not the same thing, although they frequently are equated and confused. In this volume, we address ourselves primarily to schooling, although for the moment the emphasis here is on education.[10]

The proper study for men is man—not just the shrinking physical entity that is man, but mankind. "If mankind is defined as the sum of all human beings, born or to be born into the world,"[11] then the study of mankind takes on both horizontal and vertical dimensions. Man is studied in the perspective of where and when he lives, lived, or will live—present, past, and future.

The present gives a sense of urgency. Firsthand experience with poverty, ignorance, despair, malice, bigotry, war, pollution, and prejudice must move one from mere reflection to commitment and action. The past provides perspective, an awareness that "these things, too, shall pass," without which one would forget that there have been dark clouds before and that man always has flirted with disaster. The future provides hope and faith, fresh formulations of truth, beauty, and goodness expressed through science, art, literature, and meditation, as well as a chance to apply scientific concepts to human affairs.

The central goal of education for mankind conceived in this time-binding, space-binding way is that more and more people have meaningful self-fulfillment, that more and more people are moved by the mankind imperative, that more and more people gain the perspective provided by knowledge of the past, and that more and more people glimpse what man might become—in brief, that more and more people are guided by the idea of mankind. Heaviest responsibility today for advancing such a goal rests with those who already have advanced it farthest. Heaviest responsibility tomorrow rests with the children now in our schools and, therefore, with their teachers as well.

Education is a process of developing the individual. It focuses on the individual in an effort to promote maximum self-fulfillment, but if we are to arrive at the mankind level of thought, perspective, commitment, and action, it must not stop there. Self-fulfillment must be accompanied or followed by a transcendence of self, an identification with others. There probably is no conflict between the two; it is doubtful, in fact, if true self-fulfillment is possible without self-transcendence. Consider Huxley:

> A developed human being...is not merely a more highly individualized individual. He has crossed the threshold of self-consciousness to a new mode of thought, and as a result has achieved some degree of conscious integration—integration of the self with the outer world of men and nature, integration of the separate elements of the self with each other. He is a person, an organism which has transcended individuality in personality.[12]

We know little about the nature of such a process—crossing the threshold of self-conciousness—and whether it brings with it an awareness of mankind as a whole. Does one move through a series of orderly steps from near narcissistic contemplation of self, to an identification first with nonthreatening objects and then with persons close around, to embracing a growing circle of friends and neighbors, to encompassing all mankind? Are there individual differences in this as in other human processes? Do some skip steps? Do others linger on each step as though a new stage of life? Do some, having transcended self, leap lightly from step to step as though from stone to stone in a shallow stream? These are momentus educational questions for which answers are lacking, though Kohlberg and his colleagues have made a beginning, as discussed in Chapter 3.

Nonetheless, we must not, dare not, sit back until all the answers are in. In fact, until we begin, there is no setting, no laboratory for studying the processes and deriving at least tentative hypotheses about them. One place to begin is with the formulation of assumptions from which educational programs may be planned and conducted— educational programs designed to produce conditions conducive to individual and group behavior that is compatible with the welfare of mankind.

Our first assumption is that education for mankind begins with the individual. The goal of initial forays into the environment is not to achieve a set of predetermined objectives involving mutual relations with people and things but to establish a selfhood, something set apart from other persons and things. The purpose at the beginning is not to derive meaning of "other" but to develop a sense of self. From a strongly developed selfhood comes a growing readiness to include others in meaningful ways. "Selves can only exist in definite relationship to other selves."[13]

The second assumption is that the beginning of self-transcendence (probably a lifelong process) must accompany the growing awareness of self. To linger too long over self may create a continuing need for self-indulgerce that inhibits ultimate identification with mankind. But how is the individual to be directed from self without subverting the necessary self-fulfillment? Clearly, the balance is a delicate one. The educator seeking to intervene is well advised to err on the side of delaying, rather than unduly accelerating, the shift from self to other. Again, we are without evidence, but, intuitively, it would appear easier to turn overpreoccupation with self away from self than to turn outward a personality that has not yet learned to love self. Perhaps, then, it is better at this stage of the process to go with Rousseau, letting nature do its good work in its own time, with sensitive accompanying intervention designed to reinforce the individual in a strong sense of valuing and identifying with self.

The third assumption, virtually assumed in the preceding discussion of the second, is that learning to transcend self is a developmental process, a deepening one, primarily of induction rather than of deduction. One becomes aware of variations in space, to the very small or atomic, on one hand, and to immensity, on the other. One becomes aware of depth in stepping downward or through peering into a well and, ultimately, by groping backward in time through the thin layer of human history and then to earlier beginnings. One becomes aware of certain qualities of air, flowers, and rocks, coming to ascribe concepts of perfection to things, to persons, to human relationships. Piaget has observed and described aspects of this developmental process.[14] Rigorous replications have now confirmed many of his conclusions, suggesting that there is at least some sequence involved in developing a sense of space, depth, mass, or time.[15] These findings, in turn, suggest optimal periods for various learnings, but since we do not know enough to place them in some serial order attached to age, we are well advised to intervene cautiously, avoiding arbitrary learnings in rigidly prespecified sequences. But nonetheless, the opportunities to become aware and to reflect on this awareness must be provided.

When discussion turns to intervening in learning or arranging learnings in serial order, it begins to encompass the formal educational processes called "schooling." Some assumptions applicable to both education and schooling serve as a transition to the subsequent discussion of schooling and to following chapters dealing with a mankind school and a mankind curriculum. These include assumptions of both substance and process.

An assumption about subject matter appropriate to education for mankind implicit in this and subsequent chapters is that the study of man should run like a thread through any curriculum, providing the central guiding element for selecting specific content and method. Again, we do not know what topics are appropriate at what ages. To indulge too soon or too much in man, his nature, and his deeds, or in the problems and potentialities of mankind may be to surfeit the child. However, there is now enough experience with *Man: A Course of Study,* for example, in the primary school to suggest that at least part of this subject matter can be made to have great appeal at an early age.[16] Only to study man as a biological creature, his habits, and his differences from and similarities to other creatures, although important, is not enough. In the past, this is where formal educational processes have left off, if they have reached here at all, not moving the student still farther outward from self to mankind as a whole.

Another assumption is that the learner must be involved in or introduced to raw data wherever possible: to develop a sense of space from examining differences in space, a sense of relationship from the ecological systems of ponds, a sense of things gone wrong from polluted air. Much of what cannot be experienced directly can be experienced indirectly from charts, models, filmstrips, and films, as is done so well in *Man: A Course of Study.* From these sorts of exposures, the paragraphs and pages of books follow easily, carrying one forward, backward, and outward in adventures of the mind and spirit.

It has been implied, also, on previous pages, that the learner must discover for himself, arriving at tentative principles and conclusions through reflective participation, observation, and reading. Because a mankind perspective develops slowly, the educator must exercise unusual self-discipline, resisting the temptation to provide ready-made conclusions.

The child is father to the man, becoming in adulthood what he practices most consistently in childhood and youth. The educational focus for childhood must be on the person that is becoming—the development of self within the perspective of mankind. This is what Erikson has so well defined as "ego integrity:"

> It is a post-narcissistic love of the human ego—not of the self—as an experience which conveys some world order and spiritual sense, no matter how dearly paid for....It is a comradeship with the ordering ways of distant times and different pursuits...an individual life is the accidental coincidence of but one life cycle with but one segment of history; and that for him all human integrity stands or falls with the one style of integrity of which he partakes. The style of integrity developed by his culture or civilization thus becomes the patrimony of his soul, the seal of his moral paternity of himself.[17]

In brief, the apparent duality in the goal of self-development and mankind awareness can be reduced to a unitary wholeness: the aim for each individual, in education for mankind, is finding oneself through meaningful, compassionate identification with all mankind. As is discussed in Chapter 3, a place to begin is with meaningful, compassionate identification with immediate associates.

Mankind and Schooling

The troublesome question now confronting us is what these ideas regarding mankind and education mean for the conduct of schooling. How can the school become an environment that supports the concepts and processes and fosters the commitment discussed on preceding pages? Unless mankind concepts and processes are strongly reinforced, they are likely to crumple in the face of segmental concerns in the surrounding culture.

It became increasingly clear to us, as we inquired into this problem, that changing the content of the curriculum is not enough. The possession of knowledge does not necessarily propel the individual's behavior in the direction of the meaning of that knowledge. What point is there in introducing humane and noble ideas into the curriculum if those studying them fight and bicker among themselves in the process? The idea of mankind should be pursued, therefore, in a classroom atmosphere guided by and constructed out of the very idea itself. This, in turn, means that teachers must behave in certain self-disciplined ways and not in other ways.

But schools are more than simply classrooms or what transpires in these classrooms. They are social institutions guided by assumptions and controlled by restraints which more often than not run counter to the principles presented here. In them, children are guided and molded, sometimes subtly and sometimes most explicitly, in ways that often are antithetical to the idea of mankind. More often than not, these ways are not reexamined and rethought in the light of new conditions and their effects but are passed along in the tradition of "school." The institution itself must be shaped by mankind constructs if teachers and children, in turn, are to behave according to mankind assumptions.

Our thinking led us, then, to consider the whole of schooling. Just as mankind must be considered as a unified whole and loses its very essence when atomized, the school must be viewed as a whole. But, once more, we are confronted with elusive abstractions. Although a person must be viewed as a whole or the very term becomes meaningless, we soon get down to the specifics which make up that person when we seek to describe him. And so it is with mankind and the school.

To avoid atomization to the degree possible, however, we decided to stay with the largest and most important components in describing the "mankind school." Ultimately, we developed a four-part framework to guide the creation of mankind-oriented schools (see the figure on this page). Perhaps only one of these components is relatively unique to schools: the teaching of mankind qua mankind. But even this one has had its proponents; it is the record of implementation that is sparse. The other three have enjoyed more extensive advocacy and various forms of implementation. The four are: study of the idea of mankind, teaching of conventional subject matter from a mankind perspective, emphasis on person-to-person relationships, and development of the total culture of the school as a true microcosm of mankind itself.

There is not space to develop these in detail, and so a paragraph

Dimensions of a Mankind School

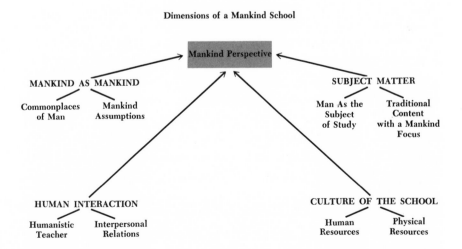

on each must suffice. They are more fully developed in Chapters 2, 3, and 4. The first, not surprisingly, proved to be the most difficult to clarify and then refine for school practice. It includes, as a minimum, man's historical search through religion for an ultimate unity, transcending while not denigrating differences among religions; attempts of nation-states to foster cultural kinship among coordinate states as a basis for peaceful coexistence and cooperation (as in China, following Confucius, down to modern times); implications of a shrinking world for one-world-mindedness; and biochemical evidence regarding *Homo sapiens* as a single species. Clearly, a major problem at this critical point in time is that at least some of the topics implied by these categories are in some places—perhaps most places—politically unfeasible so far as inclusion in the school's curriculum is concerned. And even when such topics are politically feasible and have been humanized for children's learning, formidable mysteries of transforming knowledge into relevant behavior remain.

The second—the teaching of conventional subject matter from a mankind perspective—presents at least two possibilities. One is to break out subject matter from its encapsulation in one time frame so as to open it up to analysis within another. Witness the teaching of Japan in the schools of the United States as though the former's history began with the initial establishment of communication between the two countries. There was a Japan before Commodore Perry! By studying life in Japan "before Perry," children might come to appreciate the rich past of another people coping with persistent problems long before the United States even existed. Such study could be, then, a step toward acquiring the "healthy relativism" urged by Ulich as protection against self-idolatry.

Another possibility is that of exploring a component of one's own culture in the light of its parallel or antecedent development in several others. Similarities and differences in languages, traditions, family customs, and the like come in for analysis. But this is fraught with difficulties. Chief among them is whether such comparative approaches augment or diminish appreciation and trust. It is conceivable that at least some such efforts feed prejudice and distrust.

Emphasis on person-to-person relationships has had a recent, intense resurgence in educational circles, at least in some Western countries. The group dynamics movement of the late 1940s and early 1950s emphasized one's responsibility to the group, while current approaches tend to use the group as a vehicle for reaching better self-understanding. Educational practice oriented to the mankind perspective would strive for self-understanding as an essential component of or perhaps transition to (through self-transcendence) ultimate identification with the whole of mankind. Is such self-transcendence a religious or spiritual process? Is it at all amenable to processes of systematic inquiry? Can it be taught?

The fourth part of our framework for creating schools oriented toward mankind as a unifying concept has a substantial lineage, especially with respect to schools serving some ideology. Thus, the schools at various times and in various places have been expected to exhort the virtues of Leninism or the teachings of Mao Tse-tung or "to serve as living laboratories for the teaching of democracy." The essence of our argument here, however, is that there is little point in children mouthing concepts pertaining to the brotherhood of man in a school environment shot through with prejudice; lack of respect for individuality; and distrust among administrators, teachers, children, and parents. What characterizes a school culture imbued with understanding of, appreciation for, and commitment to the idea of mankind?

To repeat, there is nothing unique about any one of these four components. It is not likely that education for mankind will be enhanced or advanced appreciably by any one pursued alone. What may be unique is the idea of infusing every component of schooling simultaneously with concern for and attention to the oneness or unity of man, with unequivocal commitment to all of the earth's people being a single species gloriously enriched by diversity. Recognizing that all of this has been said before, we are envisioning, nonetheless, a new frontier in that nothing beyond tacit willingness to tolerate diversity has been achieved before. It is a frontier for education and, therefore, for schools.

A troublesome question arises at this point. It pertains to the deliberate creation of a school and classroom environment guided by mankind values and the subsequent reinforcing effect of that environment, including the teacher, on certain kinds of behavior. Is this not just a subtle form of behavior modification dressed up in humanistic rhetoric? The answer is both "yes" and "no."

We believe that environments *do* condition the individuals in them, for better or for worse. At present, too many aspects of our unplanned societal environment are "for worse." We are saying that the environment—in this case the environment of the school—must be reconstructed "for better" and that infusing it with concepts and processes derived from the idea of mankind is "for better." Instead of allowing the school environment to emerge by happenstance, we propose that it be reconstructed from a mankind perspective. And, if you will, we propose that the individuals in that environment be "conditioned," if this is the language best describing the process, along certain lines rather than others. *But we do not intend for students and teachers to be relentlessly programmed in predetermined sequences of predetermined "right" behavior.*

One might raise the question, at this point, as to whether or not there is an element of contradiction here or, at best, of equivocation. If the "mankind way" is the way to go, why not follow through? Why not "program" children and teachers, carefully extinguishing "wrong" and reinforcing "right" behavior? There are at least two reasons for not so doing. First, while we are confident that the "mankind way" is the way to go, we are much less sure of what this means for the specifics of school and classroom learning. There are infinite possibilities here, both for viewing the idea of mankind and for conducting schooling from a mankind perspective. Second, the method suggested is antithetical to some of our basic assumptions about mankind. Meaning is a very personal thing. The individual must be a molder of his own environment, interpreting and reinterpreting it in light of the meaning it has for him. The individual is not to be thrust into a predetermined environment and called upon to conform, his conforming being appropriately reinforced to confirm it as behavior. In the mankind school, he becomes a shaper of the environment in which he participates, gradually developing a sense of potency and power as well as a deep appreciation and understanding of the consequences of his own acts—for himself, for others in his immediate environment, for mankind.

The remaining elements of our mankind school also raise many troublesome questions; these are the subject matter of subsequent chapters. Teachers and children spend hours together each day. The kind of relationship existing among them, how they treat and respond to each other, probably is more significant educationally than what they study together. We must assume that teachers are able to satisfy many of their own needs in teaching without "imposing" themselves on the children, that they are capable of disciplining themselves not to intervene as the source of all authority, that they are on the way to developing a mankind perspective. But we must not assume that these attributes are a given, because even a short period of observation will reveal this assumption to be generous indeed. Teachers require a period—probably of years rather than months—to acquire an empathy with the idea of mankind and to begin to internalize what a framework such as that presented in the figure on page 13 means for the conduct of schooling and for their teaching. This is why the teachers who conducted the experimental program described in Chapters 5 and 6 were brought into our deliberations some eighteen months before their summer effort to create a small model of a mankind school.

More questions are raised by looking at another part of our model: the curriculum. What happens to many conventional topics and themes in the curriculum when they are treated from a mankind perspective? Are there topics which are much better than others for developing the idea of human interdependence and a commitment to human welfare in general? Of course there are, but selecting the most promising topics and finding appropriate learning resources are not easy tasks, as our group of teachers found out—especially when involvement of the children themselves in this process is assumed to be an important element in a mankind school.

Likewise, reshaping the school so that its daily operation reflects a deep concern for each individual in it is so complex an undertaking that those associated with most schools simply do not try.[18] But each school has a *Geist,* a state of moral, cultural, and intellectual being which can be "felt" and sometimes described. Ironically, this state of being too frequently emerges out of tradition and the default of those who should determine it—the teachers, children, and others who inhabit the schoolhouse.

One of the best ways to assure the development of persons concerned about their society as a whole and both capable of and committed to reshaping it for the well-being of all mankind is to provide experience in such shaping from an early age. This statement reveals how we miss the point of it all. We adults—teachers, principals, parents, policy makers—establish the school environment in advance, usually by reinforcing its traditional elements. There is not much left for the child to do except, perhaps, to rebel against what impinges upon him or to conform meekly to an environment which thoughtlessly shapes him. If we really believe in the concepts and processes set forth on succeeding pages, we will begin the construction of a mankind school by giving the task to those who are to live in it.

They will have to inquire continuously into what being part of mankind means. They will need to formulate a set of mankind assumptions to live by and to revise in the light of examined consequences. They will need to think about their relationships to each other and test their ability to give and take in new situations involving persons of differing colors, habits, and religious persuasions. Children and teachers seeking to create a mankind school should question the relevance of their curriculum—and have freedom to do so. The *Geist* of their school will be the sum total of their individual and collective being at the present time of their existence—and part of the sum total of mankind.

Notes

1. W. Warren Wagar, *The City of Man,* Houghton Mifflin Company, Boston, 1963; Penquin Books, Inc., Baltimore, 1967.
2. Pierre Teilhard de Chardin, *The Phenomenon of Man,* Torchbooks, Harper & Row, Publishers, Incorporated, New York, 1961, p. 245.
3. Ibid., p. 250.
4. Robert Ulich, "The Ambiguities in the Great Movements of Thought," in Robert

Ulich (ed.), *Education and the Idea of Mankind,* Harcourt, Brace & World, Inc., New York, 1964, pp. 22-23.

5. Nathan M. Pusey, *The Age of the Scholar,* Harvard University Press, Cambridge, Mass., 1963.

6. Philip H. Phenix, "Education and the Concept of Man," *Views and Ideas on Mankind,* Bulletin 9, Council for the Study of Mankind, Santa Monica, Calif., p. 10.

7. Ulich, op. cit., p. 26.

8. John I. Goodlad, *Some Propositions in Search of Schools,* National Education Association of the United States, Washington, D.C., 1962, p. 8.

9. C. G. Jung, *The Archtypes and the Collective Unconscious,* vol. 9, *Collected Works,* Pantheon Books, Inc., New York, 1959, p. 23.

10. Some of what follows is adapted from John I. Goodlad, "The Objectives of American Education and the Interdependent World," *Indiana Social Studies Quarterly,* vol. XVIII, Winter 1965-1966, pp. 8-16.

11. Erskine McKinley, "Mankind in the History of Economic Thought," in Bert F. Hoselitz (ed.), *Economics and the Idea of Mankind,* Columbia University Press, New York, 1965, p. 2.

12. Sir Julian Huxley, in his introduction to Teilhard de Chardin, op. cit., p. 19.

13. George H. Mead, *Mind, Self, and Society,* University of Chicago Press, Chicago, 1934, p. 164.

14. Jean Piaget, *The Psychology of Intelligence,* Littlefield, Adams, & Co., Patterson, N.J., 1963.

15. Jean Piaget, *Six Psychological Studies,* David Elkind (ed.), Random House, Inc., New York, 1967.

16. Educational Development Center, *Man: A Course of Study,* The Center, Cambridge, Mass., 1968.

17. Erik H. Erikson, *Childhood and Society,* 2d ed., W. W. Norton & Company, Inc., New York, 1963, p. 268.

18. See John I. Goodlad, M. Frances Klein, and Associates, *Looking behind the Classroom Door,* rev. ed., Charles A. Jones Publishing Co., Worthington, Ohio, 1974.

Chapter 2
The Culture of the School

When an individual visits a school for the first time, he develops, almost immediately, a feeling about that school. This feeling is shaped by what he views. The hallways are empty, or they are bubbling with noise. Students sit quietly at desks, or they move about in various informal arrangements. Expressions are solemn, or there are smiles and laughter. Voices are shrill, threatening, and defensive, or they are soft, supporting, and questioning. Room and hallway environments are stark, or there is a profusion of children's work, exhibits, and plant and animal life. These factors and many more give each school a personality, a spirit, a culture. While it is not always definable, it is always discernible.

"Culture" is generally defined as the concepts, habits, skills, arts, tools, sciences, and so forth of a given society in a given time. Such concepts, habits, and the like characterize the behavior of those who make up the society. As with any "society," the school has a culture, but beyond outward signs such as activity, furniture arrangement, facial expressions, voice tones, and the presence of exhibits, what are the factors composing the culture of the school? More specifically, the question is: What is the culture of a mankind school?

We postulate that the culture of the school results from five distinct but interrelated elements: (1) the "institutional" view of man, (2) the purposes the school is attempting to accomplish, (3) the climate of the school, (4) the organization of the school, and (5) the behavior of those in leadership positions in the school.

This chapter examines each of these elements of school culture, discussing each in terms of its contribution to the establishment of a mankind culture for schooling.

The Institutional View of Man

We no longer view man as being all evil or all good, as totally rational or totally irrational. We know that he is capable of perpetrating terrible crimes against his fellow men, but we also know that he is capable of the most noble behavior. In large measure, we acknowledge that his behavior toward himself and others is shaped by environmental forces.

Many authors·have documented the potential and actual evil of man. There is the biblical notion that man lives in original sin. From another perspective, ethologists, such as Robert Ardrey, put forth evidence to suggest that man is still instinctively a territorial animal with drives left over from his animal days.[1] Further, there are those with even more powerful and contemporary evidence drawn from such places as Nazi Germany and Vietnam who suggest that man is possessed by irrational ideas such as racism, individualism, communism, socialism, capitalism, or nationalism.[2] Unfortunately, the schools are often seen by the greater society of which they are a part as tools for the promotion and promulgation of these isms. Increasingly, however, various experiments are demonstrating how, under certain environmental conditions, individuals can be conditioned to behave either as savages or with compassion in response to certain stimuli.

Douglas McGregor, in discussing business and industry in the United States, develops the notion that as a result of their ways of viewing man, organizations develop what he calls the "self-fulfilling prophecy." Thus, people in some organizational settings become what he calls "X-minded." In an X-minded organization, people are viewed and

Behaviors Manifested in a School Staffed by X-minded People

The promotion of the dependency of children upon adults for direction and the dependency of teachers upon administrators for direction.

The utilization of extrinsic rewards and punishments such as grades for students and promotion or firing for teachers.

The emphasis upon telling, showing, and training in how to do it and in proper methods of work for both children and teachers.

The reliance upon teachers who watch children closely enough to praise good work and reprimand errors and upon supervisors who do the same to teachers.

The advancement of the belief that work, with learning as a form of work, is somehow separated from the leisure activities of both children and teachers.

The fostering of the idea that jobs and learnings are primary and must be done and that teachers and children are selected, trained, and fitted to predefined jobs and learnings.

The feeling that children and teachers need to be inspired or pushed or driven to accomplish goals external to themselves and their settings.

The assumption that children and teachers prefer familiar routines; they thrive on the "tried and true."

Behaviors Manifested in a School Staffed by Y-minded People

The promotion of the independence, self-fulfillment, and responsibility of children by teachers and of teachers by administrators.

The reliance upon intrinsic reward systems for children and teachers, such as pride in achievement, enjoyment of process, sense of contribution, pleasure of association, and stimulation of new challenges.

An emphasis upon children and teachers devising their own methods of work and gaining ever-increasing understanding of the activities in which they engage.

The building of an atmosphere in which children and teachers sense that they are respected as capable of assuming responsibility and self-correction.

The advancement of the belief that work, with learning as a form of work, is a lifelong pursuit and is inextricably interwoven with the leisure activities of both children and teachers.

The fostering of the idea that teachers and children are primary and seek self-realization; jobs and learnings must be designed, modified, and fitted to people.

The feeling that children and teachers need to be released and encouraged and assisted as they set about accomplishing their own goals.

The assumption that children and teachers naturally tire of monotonous routine and enjoy new experiences; to some degree everyone is creative.

treated as if they were inferior, lazy, materialistic, dependent, irresponsible, resistant to change, and so forth, and they become so. People in different organizational settings become "Y-minded." Here, where they are viewed and treated as responsible, independent, understanding, goal-achieving, growing, creative people, they become so.[3]

While McGregor was speaking mainly of business and industrial organizations, his words are appropriate in the consideration of other institutions and certainly apply to the institutional view of man which contributes to the culture of the school.

According to the "self-fulfilling prophecy," the X-minded school will certainly produce a different kind of person than will the Y-minded school. If we are to push toward a mankind perspective, we cannot dwell upon man's real or potential evil and/or irrationality, mythical notions at best. We cannot treat children as if they are full of evil which must be suppressed or adults as if they must be controlled if they are to accomplish their goals. We must accept the idea that man is continually moving toward individual and collective potentials, potentials which are molded and shaped by home, family, community, and school.

The institutional view of man must also recognize the needs of the individuals who make up that institution. Before the individual can transcend himself, before he can move toward achieving compatibility between his own goals and those of mankind, his own needs must be met. The school can help, or it can hinder.

One view of man's individual needs is expressed by Abraham Maslow. He suggests that man is a wanting animal—as soon as one need is satisfied, another appears in its place. Further, he sees man moving through the satisfaction of a hierarchy of individual needs.[4] At the lowest level of needs are those which are physiological—needs for food, rest, exercise, shelter, and health. Until such needs are met, those of a higher order are only mildly directive. It has become virtually a cliché to point out that a child cannot learn if he is hungry or sick, but it is worth repeating that until basic needs are met where necessary by a hot breakfast program or by a program of medical and dental services, it matters not how many textbooks are provided or which method of teaching reading is used.

When physiological needs are met, man turns his attention to his social needs—for belonging, for association, for acceptance, for friendship and love. In affluent societies, and in those which emphasize individual rights and "do your own thing," we often overlook such needs. In mankind schools, while there is an emphasis upon the development of the individual, we have to be careful not to overlook the need for activities which provide for group inquiry, collective problem solving, free time for interaction, and even "school spirit."

At a higher level there are ego needs, which usually begin to appear when physiological and social needs are satisfied. These are needs which relate to self-esteem and include such things as needs for independence, achievement, knowledge, recognition, status, appreciation, and respect. Such needs are rarely met in the typical organization, including the school. In a mankind school, meeting such needs is paramount.

At the highest level in this hierarchy are man's needs for self-fulfillment, or what Maslow calls "self-actualizing." These are the needs for realizing one's own potential, for continued self-development, and for relativity. The fact that most people put their energies into the satisfaction of lower-level needs causes the needs for self-fulfillment to remain dormant.

There is no guarantee that the development of self-actualizing individuals will lead to a world in which these same individuals become aware of, understand, and become committed to a mankind perspective. However, it does seem logical to suggest that there is no hope for a mankind perspective until men rise above a preoccupation with the satisfaction of their own personal needs.

The Purposes of Schooling

Earlier in this chapter, it was stated that schools often are seen by the greater society as tools for the promotion of irrational or divisive ideas such as racism, individualism, communism, socialism, capitalism, or nationalism. The culture of a mankind school, however, must be built through the establishment of purposes which unite rather than divide all men.

Throughout the history of man, education has served five major functions: (1) it has trained the rulers and leaders of states and nations;

(2) it has socialized children and youth to the cultural and political values of states and nations; (3) it has trained those who would fill the vocations of states and nations; (4) it has acted as custodian of children and youth while parents have been otherwise involved; and (5) it has prepared people to live a creative, humane, experiencing existence.

With the advent of the universal public education experiment—and it must yet be considered to be an experiment—the training of rulers and leaders is no longer a major purpose of schools. In the developing nations, it may remain as a short-range goal, but with the assistance of the developed nations through organizations such as UNESCO, such a goal could be accomplished within the next quarter century.

In the main, and worldwide, the purposes of universal public education are largely those of socialization, custodianship, and vocational training. In serving such purposes, schools fulfill the expectations of superordinate institutions—government, church, business, and industry—which support schools with the expressed understanding that schools will in fact serve these ends.

The most rational method known to man, at least to date, to ensure the accomplishment of his institutional purposes is to establish bureaucratic structures. Such structures are highly effective when it comes to maintaining order and control and when it comes to implementing common means to accomplish common purposes. Thus, most often, we find the public schools of the world as units within massive bureaucracies.

The implications of bureaucratic structures for the culture of the school are both obvious and subtle. It is obvious that conformity of means and ends is necessary in a bureaucracy. For this reason, we can visit school after school throughout the world and find common standards for students regardless of the interests and/or abilities of these students. Usually, such standards are expressed in terms of grade levels, and their attainment is measured by grades and standardized tests. The burden of proof is upon the individual student. He succeeds or fails; the school goes on, regardless.

Not only are standards of attainment common for all students, but so are curricula and pedagogy. State or district syllabi and state or commercial textbooks dictate how and what is to be taught. Further, in all schools, we find a proliferation of policy, rules, and regulations, a culture which dictates preoccupation with telling people what to do and how to do it. Finally, externally imposed discipline is paramount. The "good" school is the one with quiet, passive, and accepting students. In short, the purpose of schooling often becomes to maintain the bureaucratic structures of the schools as they exist—the status quo.

A fifth major purpose for education was listed above: to prepare people to live a creative, humane, thoughtful, experiencing existence. As characteristics of self-actualizing people, Maslow lists acceptance of self and others, spontaneity, problem orientation, detachment, autonomy, freshness of appreciation, self-transcendence, deepness of interpersonal relations, identification with mankind, democratic orientation, distinction between ends and means, a philosophical sense of humor, and creativity.[5] If, in our schools, our purpose is to develop a culture which places a value upon self-actualizing behavior and man's needs for self-fulfillment and identification with his fellow men, then we must begin by building other than bureaucratic structures. We must develop structures which allow us to have schools which are, as McGregor says, "Y-minded," and our present bureaucratic structures must be altered to make this possible. Rather than decisions being made by those at the top of some hierarchy to be passed down for others to implement, we need structures which will allow for participatory decision making and the establishment of a climate which facilitates rather than directs how and what decisions are made.

Operationally, in a school which is facilitating of human interactions there would be adequate time set aside for teachers to be involved collectively in dialogue. Further, that dialogue would not focus on the mechanics of schooling—on "stuffing" children into predetermined boxes. Rather, it would focus on such things as purposes of the school, the needs of individual students and teachers, the development of alternative teaching-learning strategies, and the assessment of individual and collective teaching-learning success.

In such a school, teachers in the classrooms would serve as mediators between students and environment rather than as translators of that environment for students. Rather than giving information to students through an incessant outpouring of words, teachers would raise appropriate questions and assist students in finding appropriate sources of information in and out of school. They would create teaching-learning situations which would be characterized as "controlled accidents" or "springboards." Discovery centers; learning centers; open-ended art, language, and music experiences; real measurement problems; construction activities; gaming; and student-performed science experiments are all examples of in-school teaching-learning situations which could be called "controlled accidents" or "springboards." Similarly, nature walks, census taking of various kinds, observations of jury trials or other real social phenomena, interviews, and filming are examples of appropriate teaching-learning situations outside of school.

Finally, in a facilitating school, learning experiences would be characterized by freedom, choice, self-discipline, a problem-solving orientation, and responsibility within the environment of the school and with the aid of the teacher. Students frequently would be encouraged to pursue their own interests, set their own goals, monitor their own progress and their own behaviors. The "best" teacher, in the sense of facilitating true learning on the part of students, would be the one who made the fewest decisions for students and who, conversely, provided maximum opportunity for students to make their own decisions.[6]

Political Socialization

As was stated above, a major purpose for schooling is to socialize children and youth to the cultural and political values of the individual nation. It is fulfillment of this purpose which has been most antithetical to the establishment of a mankind culture in our schools. In the United States, for example, in the early years of schooling, children are led to believe that the President rarely or never makes mistakes.[7] In later years, they are taught that the average person is more influential than churches, big companies, rich people, and policemen and about as influential as newspapers.[8] Throughout their schooling, students are thoroughly "sold" on the American system, and they are taught to avoid such things as pressure groups and conflict. Such distorted views of the real world produce a citizenry which is unable to examine ideologies rationally and which is unwilling to view the activities of its government from any form of mankind perspective.

In a mankind school, children and youth would be exposed to and participate in economic, social, and political processes, for these are the processes of men. They would experience conflict, confrontation, pressure group tactics, policy formation, and even the meaning of power. Such experience would be gained through direct participation in the affairs of the surrounding community and through role play and simulation activities within the school.[9] In addition, the content of schooling would be broadened in scope to allow students to develop a perspective which includes the consideration of all men, their resources, their ideas, their contributions, their problems. In short, those things which would go on within a mankind school would have to do with mankind and they would have to do with men.

Vocational Training

Schooling throughout the world is vocationally oriented. That is, it is oriented toward judging, sorting, and, finally, preparing individuals for jobs or kinds of jobs. Thus, from the earliest years of schooling, children are judged, sorted, and prepared for the next year of schooling. Elementary school prepares for high school, high school for college, and college for graduate school. Procedures such as tracking, streaming, grading, and examining ultimately determine who will be laborers, doctors, technicians, or teachers. The individual, as he moves through the system, has very little to say about where he ultimately ends up in the world of work. In most instances, the bright student is precluded early from learning to work with his hands. Likewise, the slower student is precluded early from learning to work with his mind.

Throughout the seventeenth, eighteenth, and nineteenth centuries, such a system served the needs of society quite well. However, modern technology and ever-changing skill and knowledge requirements in contemporary society as well as staggering mankind problems suggest that we need a new view of vocational preparation in schooling.

The most precious and underdeveloped resource in the contemporary world is man himself. A mankind school must focus upon the development of this resource. In so doing, its culture must be one which does not continually narrow human options by judging, sorting, and training. Rather, the school must focus upon providing people with options through the development of experiences inside and outside of the school which relate to the real world of work. Further, mankind schooling, at least in its later phases, would allow students to drop out of and into school as they saw fit; it would allow them to choose when they wished to begin specialized job training. One might find middle school students working as teacher aides, hospital aides, day-care center aides, environmental aides, or aides to the aged as part of their regular school experience. Later, such experiences would be extended to business, industry, agriculture, the trades, the arts, and the professions. At the post-high school level, every student would have the option of serving for a year or two in one or more programs such as Vista, the Peace Corps, or even a revitalized Conservation Corps. After such experiences, students would begin to consider career commitments. Finally, in a changing world, it will be necessary to provide lifelong career education for those who may wish to or need to change careers. Such career education should be available to persons of any age.

Charles Silberman suggests that in our schools we are guilty of "a kind of mindlessness."[10] That is, we go on allowing the schools to serve the purposes of political socialization, narrow vocational training, and the bureaucracy of schooling itself without ever questioning such purposes. In fact, as Silberman suggests, we hardly even speak of purpose in our schools.

There are those who suggest that the central purpose of schooling is the development of men who can think critically.[11] Such a notion is an admirable one, and yet for mankind schooling it does not go far enough, for, as was noted in Chapter 1, rationality includes not only thinking but intelligent action as well. If we combine these two notions, thought and action, with a mankind perspective, we can say that the central purpose of a mankind school becomes the development of the rational powers of people so that these people, in turn, will think and act with a mankind perspective.

The Climate of the School

People have needs. Organizations have purposes. The interaction of these needs and their satisfaction with these purposes and their accomplishment creates a climate which, in turn, is a major component of what is referred to as an institutional personality or culture.

Argyris, through his own research and through an extensive review of other research on organizational behavior, proposes that the needs of healthy individuals are most often in conflict with the demands of formal organizations.[12] Such conflict, in turn, causes people to behave in one or some combination of ways: (1) leaving the organization, (2) moving to a higher position, (3) adopting defense mechanisms, or (4) becoming apathetic or losing interest.

Obviously, such behaviors preclude the development of a mankind culture in an organization such as a school. As pointed out earlier, where the social, ego, and self-fulfillment needs of teachers and pupils are not met, mankind purposes cannot be attained. Similarly, when mankind purposes do not prevail, the self-fulfillment needs of teachers and pupils will not be met. In a mankind school, the climate must allow individuals to meet these social, ego, and self-fulfillment needs. Thus, while teachers would be encouraging children to be creative in their activities, the teachers, in turn, would be allowed to be creative in their approach to problems. While children would be encouraged to solve real problems, teachers, in turn, would be encouraged to make decisions which affect their teaching.

Openness

Researchers of organizational climate all suggest that there is better integration between the accomplishment of organizational purposes and the meeting of individual needs when the climate of the organization is characterized by "openness."[13] Openness, in turn, is dependent upon numerous other characteristics. Among those which we shall consider here are communication, participation in decision making, freedom, and support.

In order for people to determine their collective purposes and meet their social needs, they must engage in dialogue; they must communicate. Communication in an open organization is two-way, not just downward with administrators telling teachers and teachers telling students. It involves listening and an exchange of views and information. In a mankind school, then, one would find teachers, collectively and with students and parents as appropriate, frequently discussing the goals of the school. Further, they would discuss appropriate ways of reaching these goals and ways of organizing themselves and their resources. After they had implemented their programs, they would be found collectively evaluating their success. One of the saddest characteristics of elementary schools, worldwide, is that teachers do not talk with each other consistently about anything significant, let alone purpose. Forms of team planning, teaching, and evaluation must be encouraged.

An open climate in any organization is heavily dependent upon the degree to which each individual is involved in those decisions which affect his work. In organizations where decisions, rules, and regulations are made at the top and where procedures are standardized for those in the organization, the climate is closed. On the other hand, when an organization promotes participatory decision making and supportive interactions, the climate is open. Further, where the climate is open, there is evidence to suggest that productivity is higher.[14] The implications are clear for a mankind school. Children are to be involved in decisions about the ends and means of their own learning experiences, and teachers also make their own decisions. Curriculum and instructional strategies are not predetermined by district personnel, supervisors, principals, or even totally by teachers. They emerge as a result of teacher-pupil interaction, with teacher expertise utilized as appropriate.

Freedom, too, is a characteristic of an open climate and, thus, of a mankind school. Teachers and students are free to try something new, knowing that if they fail or only partly succeed they will not suffer recrimination from others. Failure, too, is a learning experience. Other freedoms include those of pursuing personal objectives as long as such pursuit is not harmful to others, freedom to employ all available resources, and freedom to disengage or seek privacy as desired and/or as necessary.

The maintenance of an open climate requires that the institution give various kinds of supports to its members by providing human, physical, and fiscal resources and by letting them know that they and their work are valued. A mankind school needs such things as adequate space, adequate personnel, and adequate funds available to use for the purchase of equipment and materials. The application of such resources to the teaching-learning act would be decided by teachers and learners, of course.

Organization of Schooling

Somehow schooling has to be organized to carry out its functions. Such an organization arises from how we view mankind, from the type of climate which is established in the school, and from the purposes of schooling. If we view man as becoming capable of goodness and rationality, if we work for an open climate in the school, if we hold to mankind purposes of schooling—then schooling will be organized much differently than it is at present. It will be organized to facilitate bo⁺h freedom of learning and freedom of teaching.

The purposes of schooling and the organization of school are inextricably interwoven. Where the purposes of schooling are related to covering or inculcating bodies of subject matter and to judging and sorting students, it is natural to expect that schools will be organized as graded. Content will be specified by grade level, and individual student needs, interests, or differences will be tacitly considered at best in program planning. Grades, nonpromotion, requirements, and so forth will be organizational cornerstones. These are things that are well known to contemporary schooling worldwide.

On the other hand, in a school governed by mankind purposes, one would expect to see a different organization for pupil progress. There would not be grade levels, and the focus would be upon encompassing many elements of human development in planning highly individualized programs of instruction. To accomplish this, schools would be organized into broad phases, with students "flowing" through such phases as needed. Each phase would embrace a three- to four-year period of time, and each would be overlapping as individual student needs dictate.

In the early childhood phase of schooling (from ages 3 or 4 or 5 or 6) relations with peers, adults, and things in the environment and command of oral communication skills would be stressed. Children would progress at differentiated rates with the teacher exercising great freedom in providing a range of activities designed to promote motor coordination in one child and symbolic awareness in another. Skill in reading would be encouraged but would not be the criterion of adequacy for the child's progress through the early childhood phase.

In the lower elementary phase (from 5 or 6 to 8 or 9), the previous emphasis would now become secondary. Skill in reading, writing, and expression would become primary with the school's resources mobilized accordingly. Whether the child deals with this or that body of content probably is much less important than we have previously believed, so long as what is studied leads him down inherently interesting and provocative paths. The teacher could exercise great latitude, then, in the selection of substance so long as the child's basic skill development was diagnosed and enhanced. Instructional differentiation would exist both in rate and in kind.

In the upper elementary phase of schooling (from ages 8 or 9 to 11 or 12), the products of earlier emphases would become means and would be regarded as ends only temporarily when diagnosis revealed the need for correction or further refinement. Stress on independent learning and strategies of inquiry would become primary. There might be, at any given moment, as many different activities underway as there were children in the room, with tasks varying in kind and in complexity. The development of cognitive abilities and the exploration of mankind values would take precedence over the possession of any specific bodies of information.[15]

In the middle school phase of schooling (from ages 11 or 12 to 13 or 14), exploration and awareness would become uppermost while development of cognitive abilities would be deepened. Awareness of one's own interests, attitudes, abilities, and physical makeup would be paramount. In short, self-understanding would be nurtured and the role of guidance increasingly would be personalized. Exploration of others, socially and intellectually, and exploration of the physical, natural, and societal environment would be encouraged. Such exploration would be carried out through inquiry, with the student assuming more and more responsibility for decisions about such inquiry based upon his own interests, motivations, and needs.

In the high school phase of schooling (from ages 13 or 14 to 16 or 17), awareness, exploration, and individual quest would be broadened and deepened, but exploring relationships and planning and implementing courses of action would become paramount. Cultural, social, economic, and political systems would be taken apart and examined for needed improvements. The humanities, arts, and philosophy would be explored in depth for their expressions of love, pain, and humanness. Planning for the future, both for the student himself and for man collectively, would be carried out, and action would be encouraged and practiced. Activities would take place both within the school and outside of the school, with involvement in the community.

In the post-high school phase of schooling (from ages 16 or 17 to 19 or 20), awareness and knowledge of mankind values and problems would be applied to student-selected mankind work and learning. Students would take part in action programs directed at aiding the poor, the needy, the sick, the aged, and the very young in their own nation and in other nations of the world. Such work would involve total immersion in the culture of the surrounding area and would utilize a variety of skills learned in earlier phases of schooling. The key concept is service to mankind.

In the continuing life phase of schooling (from ages 19 through retirement years), students would attend school as their own needs and desires dictated. They could specialize in some vocation or avocation, or they could set as their goal cultural or personal enrichment. Students might wish to gain more and more specialization in a given field, or they might wish to change careers frequently. The important feature of this phase of schooling is that it would be available to all, regardless of economic circumstances. Continuing education as a lifelong endeavor is a goal of mankind schooling.

Organization for Teaching

In a mankind school, teachers would work together cooperatively and in teams. This "teaming" would be based upon the interests, competencies, and preferences of those making up the teams. It would be extremely flexible, ranging all the way from two teachers working cooperatively on instructional plans for a given group of students at the primary phase of schooling to a large and highly structured team of teachers with differentiated roles in a given subject area at the secondary phase of schooling.

The functions of teams of teachers would be to determine purpose, to teach together collaboratively, and to evaluate with each other their own successes and failures and those of students. The overriding function of "teaming" would be to provide those working in the school the facilitating climate and structures for participatory decision making discussed earlier in this chapter.

Teams of teachers would be made up not only of certified persons known as "teachers." Older students, parents, those learning to be teachers, and auxiliary people of all kinds also would be employed. Further, members of the community would be utilized as appropriate wherever possible. One might envision a skilled musician, a carpenter, a banker, a doctor, or a dressmaker used here or there in one team or another. The possible configurations of teams of teachers are limited only by the imaginations and creativity of those who have the basic responsibility for organizing the school. In a school with a mankind culture there are few, if any, limitations on the skills which are brought to bear on the teaching-learning act.

Environmental Factors

School organization is not concerned only with the grouping and progress of students and the working relationships of teachers. Time, material, and space are important factors to consider in the creation of an organization that will facilitate mankind purposes.

There is a tendency on the part of many people affiliated with schooling to view time as productive only when it is used by teachers to "do something to" students. There is also a tendency to compartmentalize what is done into periods of time. Thus, the bell schedule becomes the most important organizing feature of the school.

In schools with a mankind culture, time would become a much more flexible commodity, to be used with human discretion and not to direct human behavior. Thus, in such a school, we would see students and teachers planning together for long-range and short-range activities. There would be time for reflection, for enjoyment, for task accomplishment, for learning. For teachers, there would be time for dialogue and for planning.

In a mankind school there would be an abundance of material and equipment. Books, art supplies, musical instruments, construction tools and material, audiovisual and other electronic equipment, equipment for physical development, and the like would abound as the needs and interests of the school dictated. Such materials and equipment would be selected by those in the school and would be easily accessible to all.

Finally, the school plant itself would be conducive to the creation of a mankind culture. What is needed is "malleable space" which is colorful, airy, spacious, and flexible, and which breaks out of the "egg-crate" style so characteristic of contemporary school construction. "One remaining chance to blend form, line, color, and material in useful works of lasting architectural beauty is in the construction of public buildings.... Schools should be anything but a reminder of the squalid, fear-ridden existence many children live outside of school."[16]

There are those who will argue with the notions of lifelong education; with the involvement of many in schooling; with the provision of time, material, and facilities. They will talk of cost. Such people will miss the point, however. The overarching notion in a mankind world is that the most valuable resource in that world is man himself. To commit oneself to a substantial investment in mankind schooling is to take a giant step toward committing oneself to the idea of mankind.

Leadership

Each school has one person whose role it is to lead. The manner in which this individual approaches his various tasks goes a long way toward determining the culture of the school. Leaders, simply because of their designation as such, have power over other members of the school in the form of position, salary, approval, prestige, discipline, and even affection. Frequently, this power is used in a paternalistic or coercive manner. The result, most often, is acquiescence rather than self-actualizing behavior on the part of others.

In a mankind school, the leader's main function is to work toward the establishment of a mankind culture, to allow the entire school to move in the direction of "becoming." The leader must set a mankind example. That is, he must demonstrate that he holds a mankind view, that he is concerned with self-fulfillment and not his own ego needs, and that he is guided by purposefulness. By treating others as responsible, independent, and growing, he will set a model which can be emulated in a movement toward a mankind perspective.

The climate of a school is heavily dependent upon leadership. Where the leader makes most of the decisions, where he dictates what is to be done, and where he is aloof from active group participation, the climate will tend to be closed. In such a school there will be little integration between the social-emotional needs of the staff and the purposes of the school. On the other hand, where policy is a matter for group discussion, where consensus is the decision-making mode most often used, where division of tasks is left to the group, and where leadership acts emerge from the group as needed, the climate will be open. In such a school there will be a high degree of congruence between the needs of the individual and the purposes of the organization.

The leader in a mankind school focuses his attention upon facilitating the decisions of others. He provides the time, space, and atmosphere wherein such decisions can be made. In addition, he serves as a resource person. This does not mean that he has all of the answers, but rather that he knows where information is available both within and outside of the school and he can bring it to bear as those within the school identify a need for it. The leader also supports and facilitates the work of others and removes roadblocks which can cause unnecessary work for the staff. For example, he can diminish constraints by such methods as establishing release-time days, providing materials and equipment and clerical help, giving extra pay for summer work, minimizing preparations, offering freedom from regulations, and even deleting outdated curricula.

People use their resources optimally when they feel they are working in a situation that allows them freedom of trial. Freedom means being involved in the processes and decisions that influence your own work; it means being allowed the opportunity to take risks without fear of failure. The leader who builds an atmosphere of freedom also has the task of developing a parallel atmosphere of responsibility in which rational procedures of decision making and problem solving are used. When rational means are used, failure can contribute to knowledge. The leader, then, must work toward the establishment of a culture in which people are free to utilize rational means.

The leader can assist others as they move toward the establishment of rational problem-solving behavior by being aware of the steps involved in that behavior and by asking questions which lead others toward such behavior. Questions such as "Is that really the problem?" "Who is affected by that problem?" "Are there any other solutions to the problem?" "Is that the best alternative to use in solving the problem?" and "Is that consistent with our view of mankind?" will lead others to think more rationally and still allow them freedom of choice. How much closer to a mankind view is such an approach than one which involves telling people how to solve their problems!

Leadership, then, is critical to a mankind school. Through personal example, through the conscious establishment of rational problem-solving procedures, through the development of an open climate which facilitates the freedom of others to make decisions for themselves, through appropriate use of influence, and through support of others, the leader shapes the appropriate culture in that subunit of mankind in which he has influence and responsibility, the school.

A Mankind Culture

The concept of mankind is a difficult one to grasp. It seems almost beyond definition. Similarly, the concept of a mankind culture in schools is also difficult to grasp. It is a condition under which a school must operate if it is to develop children and youth who, in turn, have a commitment to mankind.

The elements which make up this suggested culture have been listed as (1) a view of people which says that they are capable of goodness and rationality and that individually they can be self-actualizing; (2) concern by all for mankind purposes; (3) a climate which allows people to become and to concentrate on mankind purposes; (4) an organization which facilitates a mankind view, mankind purposes, and openness; and (5) leaders who establish a mankind culture in schools. The underlying notion is that as schools take on such a culture, so will all of mankind come to hold a mankind view.

This brings us to the consideration of one final dimension of culture, capacity for institutional change. John Gardner has said: "a...reason men make the same mistake over and over is that they fail to recognize certain tendencies intrinsic in human institutions. All social institutions decay and rigidify and tend sooner or later to smother individuality. This is particularly true of modern, highly organized societies, capitalist or communist. Many of the attributes most galling to critics of our own system are equally characteristic of every modern large-scale society and will be increasingly so."[17]

Gardner points out that we spend our time repairing our institutions. Our schools provide an example. We try diligently to improve reading programs, vocational education programs, and the like. We move to extend the system downward to early childhood years. We pour money into giving heretofore deprived populations an equal opportunity in the existing system. Yet we do little, if anything, about making our schools self-renewing.

The true task, as Gardner sees it, is to design institutions capable of continuous change and renewal. He calls for schools in which there is reliance upon intrinsic reward; where those in the school design their own methods of work; where there is continual dialogue about purpose; where children and youth are exposed to and participate in real economic, social, and political processes; and where leadership releases and encourages people rather than controls them. It is such schools which will be capable of change and renewal. It is also such schools which will serve as cornerstones for the development of an overarching awareness of and commitment to mankind and a mankind world.

Notes

1. Robert Ardrey, *The Territorial Imperative,* Atheneum Press, Inc., New York, 1966, p. 6.

2. Max Lerner, "The Discovery of the 'Irrational': Personal and Collective," in Warren G. Bennis, Kenneth D. Benne, and Robert Chin (eds.), *The Planning of Change,* Holt, Rinehart and Winston, Inc., New York, 1961.

3. Douglas McGregor, *The Human Side of Enterprise,* McGraw-Hill Book Company, New York, 1960, and *Leadership and Motivation,* The M.I.T. Press, Cambridge, Mass., 1966.

4. Abraham Maslow, "A Theory of Human Motivation," *Psychological Review,* vol. 50, 1943, pp. 370-396.

5. Abraham Maslow, "Self-Actualizing People: A Study of Psychological Health," reprint published by the Institute for Child Study, University of Maryland, College Park, 1953.

6. Adapted, in part, from James B. Macdonald, "An Example of Disciplined Curriculum Thinking," *Theory into Practice,* vol. 6, October 1967, pp. 166-171.

7. Fred I. Greenstein, *Children and Politics,* Yale University Press, New Haven, Conn., 1965.

8. Robert D. Hess and Judith V. Torney, *The Development of Political Attitudes in Children,* Aldine Publishing Company, Chicago, 1967.

9. For a good article on sources of classroom simulations and how to prepare them, see R. Garry Shirts, "Simulations, Games and Related Activities of Elementary Classrooms," *Social Education,* March 1971, pp. 300-304.

10. Charles Silberman, *Crisis in the Classroom,* Random House, Inc., 1970.

11. Educational Policies Commission, *The Central Purpose of American Education,* National Education Association of the United States, Washington, D.C., 1961.

12. Chris Argyris, *Personality and Organization: The Conflict between System and the Individual,* Harper & Row, Publishers, Incorporated, New York, 1957.

13. See, for example, Robert Presthus, *The Organizational Society: An Analysis and a Theory,* Alfred A. Knopf, Inc., New York, 1962; and Andrew W. Halpin and Don B. Croft, *The Organizational Climate of Schools,* U.S. Office of Education, Washington, D.C., 1962.

14. Rensis Likert, *New Patterns of Management,* McGraw-Hill Book Company, New York, 1961.

15. The first three phases of schooling are described in John I. Goodlad, "Diagnosis and Prescription in Educational Practice," in *New Approaches to Individualizing Instruction,* Educational Testing Service, Princeton, N.J., 1965, pp. 27-37. A report of a conference, May 1965.

16. John I. Goodlad, *Some Propositions in Search of Schools,* Department of Elementary School Principals, Washington, D.C., 1962.

17. John W. Gardner, "Correcting Society's Specific Defects No Longer Enough to Meet Changes," *Los Angeles Times,* Sunday, Dec. 1, 1968, "Opinion" section.

Chapter 3

Human Relations
in a Mankind School

Casting the culture of the school in a mankind mold is only a beginning, for it is what happens within the walls of the individual classroom that has direct impact on the students. Here the responsibility is the teacher's.

Previous attempts to bring about a mankind awareness in students have focused their efforts on changing or expanding the subject matter offered. This is, indeed, important in establishing a mankind school and will be dealt with in the next chapter. Yet the most significant part of a curriculum is often not found in a textbook or even intended. The knowing teacher will be quick to admit that, frequently, much that is learned by students was not laid out in a lesson plan. This happens because persons coming into a classroom carry with them so much of what is personal. Background experiences, personality traits, biases, and prejudices are not left at the classroom door. Instead they are brought into the classroom and intermingle to create its total ecology. As students and teachers interact, congruence, congeniality, or conflict results. The life-style of each individual is affected by this interaction and its consequences. New insights are gained; new prejudices are formed. An altered view of self and others may be generated which has the potential for radically changing an individual's outlook and decision-making processes. This is the stuff of which schooling is made.

For those of us entrusted with the task of teaching the young not only to survive but also to contribute meaningfully to the solution of mankind problems, the responsibility is not light. Once, perhaps, we could content ourselves with helping children achieve some proficiency in the basic skills represented by the three R's, but the rate of social change and the mounting tensions of present-day living demand that we give attention not only to the cursive and computational skills but also to those underlying the nature and quality of man's relationship to man.

> If we are interested in influencing children's behavior, we shall continue to fail so long as we rely upon cognitive instruction alone. Cognitive knowledge is a powerful asset, and a prerequisite to much of human action. In the present curriculum, however, we seem to have behaved as if cognition determined behavior. Knowledge is always a means to an ultimate end. These ultimate ends, however, are not derived from pure thought; instead, they are the product of reason and emotion, cast in the form of values. Hence if the school is to truly influence behavior, it must concern itself with the broader range of feeling, thinking, and valuing.[1]

Man and Values

In Chapter 1, it was asserted that the hope of the future lies in education guided by a mankind perspective. The statement was also made that such education requires a new concept of human rights, a new understanding of freedom, and development of a new morality. We are aware of the gravity of what we suggest, for to do what we advocate is to tinker with the fundamental underpinnings of human relationships. Yet if reshaping the subprocesses of man-to-man interaction is the key to deliberately and ultimately shaping mankind itself, there is no other way. The mankind school, therefore, can ill afford to neglect the quality and tone of the human interaction which occurs within its walls. However, the quality and tone of human interaction are closely linked to the values held by the people involved.

As individuals, human beings are landlords of their own life space. Within this domain of self, the individual attempts to deal with the physical and intellectual aspects of his own organism and the tensions created as he interacts with other human beings. Within his life space, each individual lives with himself and manufactures whatever psychological devices are necessary for him to continue to ward off the intrusions and discomfort of anxiety. As input is sorted, the individual either accepts, rejects, or holds in abeyance for future reference the data coming from external stimuli. In this personal psychological realm new concepts are screened and integrated to reorganize or recreate a life-style. Thus, in the interaction of intellect and will learning takes place regardless of whether it is accidental or intentional.

When learning is viewed this way, it is not difficult to see the classroom as an arena in which human interaction generates a variety of intellectual and affective dynamics radically affecting both students and teacher. A person's actions generally have a purpose or goal sought with at least some degree of consciousness. In meaningful human involvements, actions do not occur in a disconnected or random fashion so that they contradict each other. Rather, people, either singly or collectively, move toward an end, they tend to regulate their actions in such a way that the movement is comfortable and coordinated for the achievement of a specific goal. Most people do not recognize that their interactions are governed by a directing set of guidelines which causes particular modes of action to be chosen while others are rejected. Yet this is very much the case. Such individual guidelines spring from what is referred to as man's "value framework," which may or may not be well defined. This framework, unique for the most part to each individual, embodies those various beliefs which a human being accepts as being viable and right for him. In accord with these beliefs, and in the light of current circumstances, a human being determines the quality of his human interaction and produces a rationale having the potential for at least partially explaining his behavior.

When individuals with similar value structures join in common endeavor, group activity is monitored by the common value structure. Such a framework is essential to creation of a national or individual conscience, for it provides rules against which the desirability or the rightness of action can be determined and allows the individual or nation to determine whether certain actions or judgments will be amoral, moral, or immoral. In short, if an individual or group has such a value framework well developed and operating, it will provide criteria for determining the degree of morality which can be attributed to behavior. Whether such behavior is ultimately good or bad is a matter of perception, which will be closely linked to what the judging culture, society, or religious denomination holds as good and acceptable. Thus, the nature of involvement of one human with another, of one nation with another, will be determined, to a large degree, not simply by what academic or technical skills human beings have or their culture transmits but, rather, by the value backdrop against which individuals or nations act.

The implications for creation of a mankind value framework are obvious. As children and teacher interact in pairs, in small groups, or as a class, conditions must be such that the humans involved see good in identifying with each other and experience reinforcing pleasure in the process. Having made an assessment of just where each stands in his moral development, the mankind teacher must seek to open new opportunities for identification and discussion of value positions. Ultimately, each student must be helped to step figuratively behind the eyes of his teacher and classmates to see the world from their vantage points. When this happens, the individual transcends the confines of his personal value system to at least recognize the existence of other value systems with their differing dimensions. In this act, the recognition of diversity becomes a reality and its acceptance a possibility. All of this is very personal and derives from the interaction of human with human in a supportive environment.

Teaching Values

In the traditional classroom setting, teachers have attempted to develop values in their students (1) by setting an example by direct intent or indirectly by praising good models of the past or by rewarding peer models, (2) by persuading or convincing by pointing out the advantages and "good" involved in the espousal of one set of values as opposed to another, (3) by limiting choices in offering only what is known to be palatable to children as the proper way to go, (4) by using rules and regulations to create a mold for the child until such rules are deeply embedded in activity and accepted as the only "right way," (5) by presenting a set of values as unquestionably good and held by all worthwhile human beings, (6) by appealing to conscience with the direct implication that one should feel guilt for holding another view or acting in a way contrary to what is proposed.[2]

Unfortunately, the traditional means of teaching values have not been highly successful. Perhaps the most dramatic example of this failure is religious training. Children are taught to parrot maxims such as the Golden Rule but are seldom seen to act accordingly. In fact, studies of how children assimilate such instruction reveal the failure of these methods. Selman asked children to repeat the Golden Rule, and most could do so. However, when asked what they would do if someone came up and hit them, most ten-year-olds replied, "Hit him back, do unto others as they do unto you."[3]

How, then, can the school influence children's value structures in a mankind direction? The first step is to understand how values are formed.

Value Formation

In one attempt to understand values, Kohlberg and his colleagues have described value formation as a developmental process. They have conducted longitudinal studies of children in places as widely separated as the United States, Great Britain, Taiwan, Yucatan, and Turkey and found universal stages of moral development which all children go through regardless of their culture. The stages are sequential in that a child proceeds through them in order and does not skip steps or regress, though at any one point a child's value system may be a combination of adjoining stages.

The stages are:

Stage O: Premoral Stage

Neither understands rules nor judges good or bad in terms of rules and authority. Good is what is pleasant or exciting, bad is what is painful or fearful. Has no idea of obligation, should, or have to, even in terms of external authority, but is guided only by can do, and want to do.

Preconventional Level

At this level the child is responsive to cultural rules and labels of good and bad, right or wrong, but interprets these labels in terms of either the physical or the hedonistic consequences of action (punishment, reward, exchange of favors) or in terms of the physical power of those who enunciate the rules and labels. The level is divided into two stages:

Stage 1: The punishment and obedience orientation. The physical consequences of action determine its goodness or badness regardless of the human meaning or value of these consequences. Avoidance of punishment and unquestioning deference to power are valued in their own right, not in terms of respect for an underlying moral order supported by punishment and authority (the latter being Stage 4).

Stage 2: The instrumental relativist orientation. Right action consists of that which instrumentally satisfies one's own needs and occasionally the needs of others. Human relations are viewed in terms like those of the market place. Elements of fairness, reciprocity, and equal sharing are present, but they are always interpreted in a physical or pragmatic way. Reciprocity is a matter of "you scratch my back and I'll scratch yours," not of loyalty, gratitude, or justice.

Conventional Level

At this level, maintaining the expectations of the individual's family, group, or nation is perceived as valuable in its own right, regardless of immediate and obvious consequences. The attitude is not only one of conformity to personal expectations and social order, but of loyalty to it, of actively maintaining, supporting, and justifying the order and of identifying with the persons or group involved in it. At this level, there are two stages:

Stage 3: The interpersonal concordance or "good boy—nice girl" orientation. Good behavior is that which pleases or helps others and is approved by them. There is much conformity to stereotypical images of what is majority or "natural" behavior. Behavior is frequently judged by intention: "He means well" becomes important for the first time. One earns approval by being "nice."

Stage 4: The law and order orientation. There is orientation toward authority, fixed rules, and the maintenance of the social order. Right behavior consists of doing one's duty, showing respect for authority, and maintaining the given social order for its own sake.

Postconventional, Autonomous, or Principal Level

At this level, there is a clear effort to define moral values and principles which have validity and application apart from the authority of the groups or persons holding these principles and apart from the individual's own identification with these groups. This level has two stages:

Stage 5: The social-contract legalistic orientation. Generally with utilitarian overtones. Right action tends to be defined in terms of general individual rights and in terms of standards which have been critically examined and agreed upon by the whole society. There is a clear awareness of the relativism of personal values and opinions and a corresponding emphasis upon procedural rules for reaching consensus. Aside from what is constitutionally and democratically agreed upon, the right is a matter of personal values and opinion. The result is an emphasis upon the legal point of view, but with an emphasis upon the possibility of changing law in terms of rational considerations of social utility, (rather than rigidly maintaining it in terms of Stage 4 law and order). Outside the legal realm, free agreement and contract is the binding element of obligation. This is the "official" morality of the American government and Constitution.

Stage 6: The universal ethical principle orientation. Right is defined by the decision of conscience in accord with self-chosen ethical principles appealing to logical comprehensiveness, universality, and consistency. These principles are abstract and ethical (the Golden Rule, the categorical imperative) and are not concrete moral rules like the Ten Commandments. At heart, these are universal principles of justice, of the reciprocity and equality of the human rights, and of respect for the dignity of human beings as individual persons.[4]

A child's stage of development can be determined through analysis of his responses to a series of moral dilemmas. For example, a child is asked,

"Before the Civil War, we had laws that allowed slavery. According to the law, if a slave escaped he had to be returned to his owner like a runaway horse. Some people who didn't believe in slavery disobeyed the law and hid the runaway slaves and helped them to escape. Were they doing right or wrong?"

At Stage 1, an answer reflects a punishment and obedience orientation:

"They were doing wrong because the slave ran away himself; they're being just like slaves themselves trying to keep 'em away."

Instrumental relativity can be seen in a Stage 2 response:

"They would help them escape because they were all against slavery. The South was for slavery because they had big plantations and the North was against it because they had big factories and they needed people to work and they'd pay. So the Northerners would think it was right but the Southerners wouldn't."

At Stage 3, the following response indicates the importance of approval, affection, and helpfulness:

"If a person is against slavery and maybe likes the slave or maybe dislikes the owner, its O.K. for him to break the law if he likes, provided he doesn't get caught. If the slaves were in misery and one was a friend he'd do it. It would probably be right if it was someone you really loved."[5]

Implications for Teaching

Assuming that values are formed through a developmental process, Kohlberg defines the aim of moral education as "the stimulation of the next step of development rather than indoctrination into the fixed conventions of the school, the church, or the nation."[6] Such stimulation is accomplished through a kind of Socratic dialogue with children in which the teacher presents a moral dilemma to a child or group and systematically supports and clarifies responses a level above the stage the children are at.[7] An experimental trial of this method with twelve children who ranged from Stage 2 to Stage 4 found that after twelve weeks a majority had advanced almost a full stage. Retesting a year later revealed that the children retained the advance.[8]

Other methods of teaching values are also available. For example, Raths and his associates suggest that the way to begin teaching values is by concentrating on teaching students the *process* of valuing, wherein it is assumed that values are personal and are of little worth unless freely accepted and allowed to penetrate the life-style of the person who holds them.[9] Such a process, however, demands a new kind of relationship between teachers and students. No longer, according to Raths, would the master be seen as having the truths to be handed down to the thirsty students. Rather, the new approach would demand a relationship which views the questioning process as a task to be undertaken mutually and simultaneously. The role of the teacher becomes that of providing new experiences for children so that they become aware of alternative modes of action. More succinctly, the teacher's role is to provide a richness of experience which may facilitate change in the child.[10] Presumably, these experiences would provide the foundation for an examination of the students' view of themselves and the people around them. The attempt would clearly be to set the stage for what has been referred to as the "Aha" experience of education,[11] in which the student, having been confronted by a series of colliding circumstances, suddenly achieves a new insight. Such insights once grasped and preserved as norms for determining the good of future actions form a moral construct.

The Teacher's Role

For better or worse, social realities come to school with the children, the teacher, the administrator, and the supervisor.[12] The values, pressures, and conflicts of the culture have an impact on each and become incorporated into personalities in such a way that human actions, reactions, and decisions cannot remain unaffected. In the case of the teacher, his social background and personal history constitute the screen through which he views the world and selects and arranges experiences for children. None of his daily decisions escapes the influence of the emotional satisfactions which he finds in his relationship with his colleagues, in his family life, or in his adjustment to universal human problems. An essential prerequisite for the mankind teacher, therefore, is that he have some idea of just where he is at within his own being. To use the often-quoted Socratic phrase, he must "know himself." He must have some understanding of his own value system, his impact upon his fellow human beings, their impact upon him, and finally some sense of his own emotional response to a variety of persons and situations. He must be sensitive and dedicated to creating a relationship with students that will allow them to sense in him a firm commitment to education as a means for bringing about world peace and strengthening the bonds uniting humanity. It may be that this hard-to-describe "sensed commitment" is the crucial factor differentiating the effective mankind teacher from those who are less successful.

In what has been said above, the emphasis is largely on the characteristics exemplified by the mankind teacher. This emphasis is intentional because the teacher frequently is perceived by his students and other constituencies connected with the school as the leader responsible for building group structure and maintaining goal orientation. As such, he engages in a variety of tasks, including proposing goals for class consideration, seeking or giving information or opinions, clarifying and interpreting ideas, and summarizing data into meaningful categories, in addition to a multitude of tasks such as giving encouragement, making peace, or increasing class participation in order to keep interaction running smoothly.[13]

Inherent in each of these tasks and its accompanying roles are judgments which necessarily flow from a teacher's value framework. His view of what is right or wrong, good or bad, will manifest itself in his action and attitude as he attempts to influence students toward greater understanding. Research has pointed out that a group leader, such as the classroom teacher, is a high-status member whose opinions are influential in the formation of group opinion. It is not much of a leap to assume that he has considerable influence over the value framework eventually adopted as that of the classroom group. Additional research underlines the fact that groups do apply formal and informal social pressures to group members to cause their behavior to conform to the group standards which set limits for acceptable behavior. Obviously, then, the human interaction of the classroom actors has the potential for radically affecting at least a limited portion of a student's value system.[14]

This is not to suggest, however, that identical values will be the certain result. As two or more humans impinge upon each other's life space to form groups, the resulting interactions do hold potential for producing a similar realignment of internalized knowledge to form values and norms. However, although individual values influence formation of group values (and vice versa), complete congruence of group values with the values of individuals in the group is not usually found. The degree to which individuals can tolerate deviation by the group from personal values will vary. Thus, it is possible for individuals to claim membership in a class, religious denomination, or society without complete acceptance of the group's values. In the same way, a group can tolerate some degree of individual value deviation among its members. Generally, however, the deviation cannot be too radical without causing alienation. Be this as it may, individual value frameworks *are* influenced by interaction with other human beings, and group membership does legitimize and facilitate the acceptance of norms. A mankind teacher can make a conscious and specific effort to expose students to situations and experiences that will urge formation of specific value constructs. However, deviation must also be respected in accord with mankind norms.

The Teacher As Helper

This brings us face-to-face with the need for a mankind teacher to make a basic investment in what Carl Rogers some years ago referred to as a "helping relationship"—one in which one of the participants intends that there should come about in one or both parties more appreciation of, more expression of, more functional use of, the latent inner resources of an individual.[15] Such a relationship assumes that the helping person, in this case the teacher, is trying to influence the individual who is being helped. The further expectation is that any change brought about in the receiver of the help will be constructive

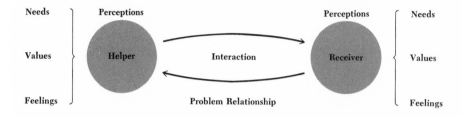

and useful to him. One might diagram such a relationship as shown above.

As useful as they are to understanding, diagrams tend to suggest structure and rigidity. In the case of the helping relationship nothing could be farther from the truth. The true helping relationship is dynamic and fluid and characterized by warm communication, both verbal and nonverbal. What the diagram points out is that both the helper and the receiver of help have needs of a biological and psychological nature which they attempt to satisfy as they interact. Each brings with him an array of feelings and a set of values. As helper and receiver approach the interaction—and throughout—each has perceptions of himself, of the other, and of the entire situation in terms of expectations, role definitions, and standards. Central to the interaction is some need or problem which may be external to the individuals, interwoven with their relationship, or actually rooted in the relationship that exists between them. The origin or focus of such a problem is really incidental. It is the relationship between the individuals that is of prime importance in a helping situation.

When the interaction begins, the receiver's needs, values, and feelings and his perception of the situation, including the problem and the helper, cause him to have a vested interest in the outcome of the interaction and the specific objectives to be achieved. The helper (teacher) likewise has certain objectives for the interaction derived from his needs, feelings, and values; his perception of them; his assessment of the situation; and his view of the receiver of help. As the interaction is played out, both the helper and the receiver exercise influence over what occurs. However, except for surface conformity or interruption of the interaction, it is the receiver of help who remains in control of whether change really takes place.

Ideally, what we see here is a high-quality, humanistic teaching-learning relationship which encompasses the basic needs of both teacher and learner and permits mutual growth to occur.

Such a helping relationship imposes new constraints upon one who seeks to teach. Translating what Rogers perceives as the essential characteristics of a helping relationship into characteristics of the humanistic teacher provides a set of guidelines. First of all, the student must see the teacher as trustworthy and dependable in the sense that the teacher's external behavior is perceived as not contradicting his internal thoughts and feelings. Children are quick to recognize the games adults play, and few things damage adult-child relationships as much as trust that has been betrayed. Also, children are sensitive to nonverbal communications and often are quick to recognize adult insincerity. The child, in addition, must see the teacher as truly interested in his endeavor; just as the teacher must be aware that he, too, can benefit from and gather new insights into the material at hand as, together, student and teacher explore what it offers.

The mankind teacher must be aware of his personal shortcomings and yet be strong enough to maintain his integrity. No teacher is less successful than the one who has not assessed accurately his own understanding of the subject matter and who is unwilling to admit that he does not have all the answers for fear of losing face. Related to this is the need for a humanistic teacher to be seen as accepting of divergent points of view or at least allowing for deviancy. As such, the teacher will not demand conformity to a stated position but will accept the student as another human being who must be allowed the freedom to question and to maintain his own individuality in creativity and communication. Such a teacher will display true empathy so that he is seen as sincerely attempting to enter into the student world of feelings and personal meanings to see things from a student point of view. Finally, the humanistic teacher is perceived as attempting to free the student from external threat and fear so frequently associated by children with school. This involves effort to free the child from the negative aspects of evaluation and grading, as well as effort to help the child to deal with his internal feelings and conflicts which he finds threatening within himself. Underlying all of this the teacher must view students as in the process of becoming—a state not far different from his own.

Rogers holds that learning will be facilitated if a teacher's external behavior reflects his true thoughts and feelings. This demands that the teacher consistently put aside false facades and expose himself to his students as he really is. He must be aware of his own attitudes and accepting of his own feelings. Once these goals are reached, he will become a "real person." He can be enthusiastic about subjects he likes and bored by topics he does not like. He can be angry, but he can also be sensitive or sympathetic. Because he accepts his feelings, he has no need to impose them on his students or to insist that they feel the same way. He is a person, not a faceless embodiment of a curricular requirement or a sterile pipe through which knowledge is passed from one generation to the next.[16]

Rogers's work is not without support from the field. In the process of analyzing humanistic teaching, a task force of teachers at the University Elementary School, University of California, Los Angeles, set about listing the characteristics they felt were essential for humanistic teachers. In their initial attempt, they came up with thirty-nine characteristics which were subsequently distilled to the following list closely resembling Rogers's conceptualization: The humanistic teacher (1) is fair and honest; (2) is open-minded; (3) is flexible; (4) is stable emotionally; (5) cares about children and comes across as real; (6) trusts children and is not suspicious; (7) carefully listens to children; (8) is aware of his own feelings; (9) communicates and is aware of the children's feelings; (10) is aware of personal impact upon others; (11) builds upon the individual spirit of the child; (12) focuses on the child's process of growth; (13) does not negate, humiliate, or belittle children, but rather creates a positive feeling in the child; and (14) helps children to live up to their potential. Subsequent discussion of these characteristics with students seemed to substantiate them as being desirable in the context of the student-teacher interchange.

Research at the University of Florida under the direction of Arthur Combs also tends to substantiate the description of the helper. These studies consistently indicated that effective helpers saw people from the inside rather than from the outside. They were more sensitive to the feelings of students and were more concerned with people than things. They saw behavior as caused by here and now perceptions and environment rather than by historical facts. They saw others and themselves as able, worthy, and dependable. They saw their task as freeing rather than controlling and as an involved and encouraging process. The one significant finding of these studies was that objectivity had a negative correlation with effectiveness as a helper.[17] It appears that there has to be some subjective involvement with the person being helped on the part of the helper.

What is brought home very forcibly from what has been said is that freedom from fear, anxiety, and pain accompanied by mutual concern appears to affect radically, for the better, the human beings involved in the teaching-learning situation. At a minimum, the prospect for learning is considerably enhanced when at least some of these elements characterize the human interaction of the classroom setting.

As was said at the outset, consistent values produce stability and constancy of action. The individual must be helped to gather to himself the moral girders that will construct a mankind framework overarching his entire view of life and the lives of those with whom he interacts. His predisposition to the consideration and acceptance of such values will be influenced, as we have pointed out, by the quality of the teacher-student interaction. But to adopt a mankind perspective and its inherent values the student must be exposed to such values in operation and to their implications for the wider sphere of living. Therefore, the teacher himself must have a commitment to the mankind perspective. The teacher-learner interaction must be humane and must be governed by the mankind values which the interaction seeks to teach, including an awareness of man's similarity to his fellow man, an acceptance of diversity, and a commitment to the obligations springing from this understanding of self and others.

In summary, then, the teacher who strives to know himself and to develop the characteristics in his interaction with pupils which correlate with those of a helping relationship built upon love will be in the best position to influence the value formation process. A teacher who chooses experiences for his students that will allow them to examine their own worth, to examine and challenge the value constructs which govern their actions, and to build mankind elements into their own value framework will best contribute to the creation of a mankind perspective among his students.

The Mankind Classroom

Unfortunately, teachers have not been trained in traditional teacher training institutions to cultivate particular kinds of relationships with students, especially those proposed in this chapter. Certification procedures stress competence in the academic disciplines, but as we have tried to point out, academic proficiency is not enough for the successful teacher of today. Attention must be paid to the way he or she interacts with students; for teaching is, after all, a process of human interaction—a process which fosters and exemplifies the tenets of a mankind perspective.

In the mankind classroom, therefore, one might expect to find the teacher interacting with the children in a free and open fashion. Differences among the children in terms of ethnic backgrounds, cultural heritage, tastes, and styles of dress would be fit topics for discussion. In these discussions, particular attention would be given to helping children to accept without condemnation the viewpoints of their peers and to value the diversity of resources that each human brings to the class. Nor would the teacher be aloof from such discussions. As the children reveal their backgrounds, likes, and dislikes, so too would the teacher expose his biases and prejudices for class commentary and question.

The organization of the classroom itself would be flexible so that groups of students could work together under a variety of conditions. Special effort would be made to give every child an opportunity to know all of the other children by restructuring work groups frequently. For example, a group of children brought together for special work in reading would be widely dispersed for an art project. Still different groups would be formed for mathematics. The impersonality of the traditional classroom with its rows of desks and spirit of isolation would be studiously avoided. As new children joined the class or a particular work group, genuine efforts would be encouraged among the rest of the students to learn what new resources were available to the group in the new child and what new fears and expectations were brought with him, and to impart a sense of value and worth to each new member. Such efforts suggest, for example, that discussions of personal feelings and thoughts not only be permissible but be fostered. Children would be encouraged to discuss among themselves and with the class as a whole their reasons for acting in a particular way or for preferring specific methods of doing things as opposed to other options.

When problems of discipline or deviant behavior arose, the teacher would provide opportunities for a child to examine the ramifications of his own activity and to receive feedback from his peers about how they perceived him. Alternative modes of behavior might be suggested in the context of a discussion of how people live together in peace and harmony and what constitutes disruption. Every attempt would be made to understand the motivation behind action and to anticipate outcomes of all options presented.

Basic to the mankind classroom would be respect for individuality and personal freedom. Students would be permitted to choose work and activities which suited their individual needs. They would be given freedom to participate in what they felt benefited them most at a particular time, but only after they had examined carefully the effects of their choices and had decided to accept responsibility for whatever the outcomes might be.

In all situations, the mankind teacher would view himself as a knowledgeable peer in the learning process to whom students might turn for relevant information or for additional options. Nothing would be viewed as unquestionable or as unfit subject matter for learning. Where conflict or uncertainty arose among students, the mankind teacher would intervene, not as a policeman or peacemaker but as a counselor to clarify the issues for student judgment. The mankind teacher would be reticent to impose punishment or restriction but would work to allow students to determine and freely choose methods of redress or compensation. When a violation of individual rights was involved, the mankind teacher would seek to expose the ramifications for the class. Again, alternative methods to achieve the same end would be examined. Above all, learning experiences would permit students to determine under what conditions personal rights and wants must be sublimated for the good of all.

In all that has been said, the assumption is made that the mankind teacher enters into classroom interactions with honesty and candor. When he is displeased, he feels free to express his displeasure and to talk about why he feels so. When children express affection and love for him, he is able to receive it and enjoy it. When confidences are shared, he treasures the trust and is likewise not fearful of trusting students. If requests come for additional time or attention, plans are made mutually to meet students' needs. Unreasonable demands are confronted honestly and resolved in a noncoercive atmosphere. When evaluations must be made, they are done individually and in a manner that permits and encourages students to give honest feedback concerning their tasks without fear of retribution. Along with the teaching of specific skills, the mankind teacher sees his role as helping students to evolve as thinking, feeling human beings who are able to see beyond the parameters of their own desires and needs to the global concerns of other men and ultimately of all mankind.

In such a classroom, humans would be exhibiting human care and concern for humans. In such an atmosphere, the conceptualization of Chapter 1 could be realized in a sincere effort to "shape" the character of the more intimate subprocesses of human interaction within the frame of a mankind reality. In such a classroom, children would come to understand mankind.

Notes

1. Louis J. Rubin, *Facts and Feelings in the Classroom,* Walker Publishing Company, New York, 1973, p. 28.

2. Louis E. Raths, Merrill Harmin, and Sidney B. Simon, *Values and Teaching: Working with Values in the Classroom,* Charles E. Merrill Books, Inc., Columbus, Ohio, 1966, pp. 34-38.

3. R. Selman, "Role Taking and Moral Judgment," in Lawrence Kohlberg and Elliot Turiel (eds.), *Recent Research in Moral Development,* Holt, Rinehart and Winston, Inc., New York, 1971.

4. Lawrence Kohlberg and Elliot Turiel, "Moral Development and Moral Education," in G. Lesser (ed.), *Psychology and the Educational Process,* Scott, Foresman and Company, Glenview, Ill., 1971, pp. 415-416.

5. Ibid., p. 444.

6. Ibid., p. 416.

7. A detailed description of the curriculum may be found in M. Blatt and L. Kohlberg, "The Effects of Classroom Discussion on the Development of Moral Judgment," in Kohlberg and Turiel (eds.), op. cit.

8. M. Blatt, "The Effects of Classroom Discussion upon Children's Level of Moral Judgment," in Kohlberg and Turiel (eds.), op. cit.

9. Louis E. Raths et al., *Teaching for Thinking: Theory and Application,* Charles E. Merrill Books, Inc., Columbus, Ohio, 1967.

10. Raths, Harmin, and Simon, op. cit., p. 47.

11. See Sidney C. Callahan, "The Aha Experience in Education," *Notre Dame Journal of Education,* vol. 1, no. 3, Fall 1970, pp. 202-207.

12. For an insightful discussion of the school as a socializing agent, see Louis M. Smith and Sally Schumacher, "The School as Socializer," in John I. Goodlad and Harold G. Shane (eds.), *The Elementary School in the United States,* 72nd Yearbook of the National Society for the Study of Education, pt. II, The University of Chicago Press, Chicago, 1973.

13. See Jerrold M. Novotney and Kenneth A. Tye, *The Dynamics of Educational Leadership,* Educational Resource Associates, Los Angeles, 1973.

14. Paul A. Hare, *Handbook of Small Group Research,* The Free Press, New York, 1962.

15. Carl Rogers, *On Becoming a Person,* Houghton Mifflin Company, Boston, 1961, p. 40.

16. Ibid., p. 287.

17. A. W. Combs et al., *Florida Studies in the Helping Professions,* Social Science Monograph 37, University of Florida Press, Gainesville, 1969.

Chapter 4
Subject Matter
in a Mankind Curriculum

Recasting the culture of the whole school into a mankind mold is largely outside the control of the single teacher. The individual teacher can, however, effect a change in the form and content of interactions with students. The previous chapter discussed the form of student-teacher interactions—the helping role a mankind teacher plays and the atmosphere of the single classroom. Here we will discuss the content—the subject matter to be taught. Subject matter in a mankind curriculum must contribute to the student's understanding of the concept of mankind and foster the development of a mankind perspective. These two goals will not just happen; they must be deliberately planned for and carefully fostered. Just as schools play a critical role in meeting these goals, the individual teacher and the subject matter offered in the classroom also bear a major responsibility.

We do not advocate discarding the traditional curriculum completely. Indeed, in a mankind school the traditional academic disciplines will continue to be a major source of subject matter. Their scope must be expanded, however, to encompass subject matter from the non-Western world. For example, the social studies and literature programs can include works by Gandhi, Confucius, Buddha, and Mao as well as Shakespeare, Chaucer, Martin Luther King, and John F. Kennedy. Also, in addition to the academic sources traditionally used as a basis for the curriculum, new sources will be added, such as the behavioral sciences and other social science disciplines not traditionally included in the curriculum: psychology, sociology, anthropology, and ethics. Thus, the basis for subject matter in a mankind curriculum is significantly expanded.

Seven criteria are suggested in this chapter to provide guidelines for selecting appropriate subject matter for a mankind curriculum. These criteria are based on eight assumptions, broad statements about the kinds of values a person with a mankind perspective would hold with regard to his fellow men. There may be other values in addition to these which are important in a mankind perspective, but those identified here would seem to be held in general agreement:

1. Human life is valued and preserved.
2. The worth and dignity of the individual are to be respected.
3. The social order must be based on justice and the rule of mankind values.
4. Human association is characterized by liberty and freedom.
5. Human expectations and personal capabilities must be fully realized.
6. Mankind conditions and values take precedence over personal desires, ambitions, and values.
7. Truth and knowledge are desired and sought.
8. A mankind ecology must be sought for the survival of human life.

In addition to forming the basis for selection of content, the mankind assumptions themselves will necessarily be included in the curriculum as a means of teaching a mankind perspective.

With these assumptions in mind, subject matter can be examined in the light of the following seven criteria to determine its utility and place in the mankind curriculum.

Criteria for Selecting Subject Matter

1. Subject matter in a mankind curriculum must contribute to an understanding of the concept of mankind.

Subject matter can contribute to an understanding of the concept of mankind by consistently keeping before students the basic attributes of man, the things he has in common, that which makes him human. We have tentatively identified five such attributes which all people share and called them commonplaces of man:

1. All people value. Values may vary from person to person, from culture to culture, or from nation to nation, but the process of valuing and objects of value exist for all people. Students may discover this through the study of ethics and philosophy by identifying universal human values which have been held by all great thinkers regardless of their time or culture. A study of religions of the world will point out that from the most primitive societies to the most advanced, people have selected objects or beings or attributes of nature which they value, esteem, and worship. Objects and beings of value have been preserved throughout history in art forms, and so the study of art, too, can contribute to the student's understanding that all people value.

2. All people have emotions. The ways of expressing the basic emotions vary, as do values, but all people no matter where they live experience love, hate, anger, frustration, joy, and sorrow. Literature can be a great resource in helping the child to experience the emotions of people in different times and places and help him to realize that they are very similar to his own. Films can portray emotions directly, whether it be a farmer in Mali happy and relieved at the coming of the rains, a Pakistani mother mourning her child lost in a flood, or a Frenchman celebrating Bastille Day. Students can be asked to identify with the emotions expressed in the music and art of all cultures.

3. All people have needs. Some needs of man are very basic to sustaining life: air, food, and water. Other needs are also rather universally recognized: need for social interaction, need for respect of self, need for organization, and need for understanding and explaining one's world. There are various ways of categorizing and

examining the needs of people, but the essential understanding for a mankind curriculum is that all people have needs which they strive to meet. The study of biology can certainly contribute to an understanding of man's basic needs. Concepts from psychology and sociology can help in the exploration of other needs of individuals and groups.

4. All people think. As a result of this capacity, man is able to change, grow, and solve problems. The ability is an inherent one, but one which needs careful development and guidance. In this capacity is man's hope for the future. Study of the evolution of man and his prehistory can explain how the ability to think set man apart from other animals and allowed him to prosper. The study of philosophy with its questions about existence and evidence from the senses can also be fascinating for students exploring this attribute of mankind.

5. All people communicate. The forms of communication can vary from situation to situation, but man as he is today depends heavily upon his ability to communicate. Common concerns, solutions to problems, growth, and change are dependent upon this ability to communicate. The subject matter which can contribute to an understanding of this attribute is almost too varied to catalog. Grammar can be treated as the basic bones of communication; the many different alphabets and forms of writing can be examined; foreign languages can be seen as ways of expanding one's own ability to communicate; and, of course, literature from throughout the world is direct communication.

With an understanding of these commonplaces, students will more closely identify with all groups of people, no matter where they are found or what their mode of living may be; they will be able to identify more closely with the unity of mankind.

2. Subject matter in a mankind curriculum must be in agreement with and support the concept of mankind and a mankind perspective.

Some of the dimensions and ideas of the mankind perspective were identified in Chapter 1. The subject matter in a mankind curriculum would need to be in agreement with and support those dimensions, and any subject matter which is not in basic agreement with a mankind perspective must be reconsidered for inclusion in a mankind curriculum. For example, any instructional materials which teach the divisiveness of man must be revised or rejected. An understanding of mankind includes the possession of a sense of unity, not separateness or superiority, among humans. Topics supporting such views as the superiority of any group of people over another, the condoning of unequal distribution of the available natural resources among a very few technologically developed nations, and the acceptance of arbitrarily imposed territorial rights of one group in opposition to another would not be appropriate subject matter for a mankind curriculum. However, the study of evolution could explain how and why differences among races such as skin color might have come about. Basic topics in biology such as anatomy and genetics could show how all humans are alike. Geography and history could explain how territorial claims have developed and show the transience of the most "unbreachable" borders.

Any subject matter which approves of or allows for inhumane action against other men must be questioned. Positions supporting the exploitation of any group by another, war as a condoned method of resolving conflict, and the denial of basic human rights to any person must be rejected as inappropriate for a mankind curriculum. The study of problems involving the divisiveness of man as they occur in our world today should most certainly be a part of a mankind curriculum, but only to understand them to be intolerable situations and, thus, to search for methods of reconciliation. The daily newspaper can be a source for discussions about the energy crisis and the maldistribution of the world's resources and the divisiveness of conflict in the Middle East, its far-ranging repercussions, and the rights and wrongs on both sides. Such studies will occur not only in a cognitive sense, but in the affective concerns of the pervasive attitudes, values, and habits implicit in them also.

3. Subject matter in a mankind curriculum must have relevance to mankind.

We have suggested that mankind is the proper study of men. Mankind must be made central to all that is included as subject matter. An essential part of subject matter having relevance to mankind is appreciation of the diversity of mankind. Understanding mankind as a concept contains no attempt to reduce all men to the lowest common denominator. Rather, it contains a recognition of and a valuing of the richness of life represented in the diversity of man and the ways in which he lives. Man, wherever he is found and the variety of ways in which he lives, must be an integral part of a mankind curriculum.

The diversity and richness of humans can be studied through units on clothing and food, through the arts, and through units on how people live throughout the world that are traditionally found in the geography and social studies curriculum. Anthropological studies could examine the various cultures of the world and point out their similarities as well as differences.

4. Subject matter in a mankind curriculum must contribute to the ability of the student to transcend himself and his culture.

If an understanding of and a commitment to mankind are to occur, Ulich suggests that students must be helped to go beyond themselves and rise above themselves.[1] A student must be helped to overcome his narrow, segmental, limited views of himself and his culture to achieve a broader view of man and his world. There appears to be a major requirement to be met, however, before self-transcendence can occur to any significant degree. Students must first be helped to understand themselves: their emotions, attitudes, values, abilities, desires, and problems. Only as a well-developed understanding of self is achieved can students truly transcend themselves and achieve an equal degree of understanding and feeling for other men. Thus, a mankind curriculum will make deliberate provisions for helping students come to know and understand themselves as well as others. It is here that psychology as a relatively new data source for the curriculum becomes heavily utilized.

A number of curriculum packages and texts are currently available on the commercial market which are designed to help students understand themselves. Examples are *About Me,*[2] *Moods and Emotions,*[3] and *Learning about Me,* a program in developing self-concept.[4]

Understanding of self is becoming an area of concern to many educators, and publishers are producing an increasing number of instructional materials to meet this new concern.

Also available on the commercial market are a number of instructional products designed to help students understand the causes and manifestations of prejudice. One such product is *What is Prejudice?*[5] An understanding of the causes of prejudice and how it is expressed may help the student in learning to transcend himself.

Literature, of course, is a classic tool for helping the student understand himself as well as others. In addition, games which require the student to role-play the characters in a story or other children in the class or even historical figures can contribute to the student's ability to "step into the other person's shoes."

5. Subject matter in a mankind curriculum must include persistent topics which are so broad and pervasive that they can be examined through a variety of perspectives.

The development of a mankind perspective and the ability to transcend oneself are, as indicated above, dependent upon the student's ability to see himself, his world, other people, and current issues and problems, alleged and real, from differing viewpoints. This includes not only presenting a balanced view—reading *Light in the Forest* in conjunction with *Drums along the Mohawk,* for example—but also choosing topics for discussion which offer many rights and wrongs and a fertile area of gray for exploration. Conflict in the Middle East, distribution and use of natural resources, and various revolutions in history can certainly be considered from several perspectives. Opposing points of view should be deliberately built in as part of a mankind curriculum. The topics are endless—nuclear energy, pollution control, capitalism versus socialism, individual freedom versus collective good—and are familiar to any teacher who has listened to things students are really interested in exploring. In such discussions, of course, it is the teacher's responsibility to ensure that all points of view are given an adequate hearing and considered on their merits.

Commercial instructional materials are also becoming available which contribute to this criterion for subject matter in a mankind curriculum. An example is the social studies program, *From Subject to Citizen.*[6] It provides students with opportunities to develop and role-play a variety of positions and characters in the historical development on the United States. *Opposing Viewpoints Library* confronts the student with varying perspectives on selected issues.[7]

6. Subject matter in a mankind curriculum must promote action based on a commitment to mankind.

As pointed out in Chapter 1, educated men do not necessarily act when others have committed grave crimes against their fellow men. The aim of the mankind school must be to foster the *rational* man who is committed to action and does not allow his wisdom and intelligence to be inactive when injustices against others are seen. The subject matter in a mankind curriculum must contribute to this goal. An intellectual understanding of the concept of mankind is not enough, even though it is an essential beginning. This knowledge and understanding must then be used as a guide to behavior and transmitted into action with regard to all men. Courses of action must be identified and followed. Collecting food and blankets for earthquake and flood victims; raising funds to provide legal assistance to the poor; providing social contacts for lonely senior citizens; getting involved in community action programs seeking improvement of urban areas; and seeking out social situations involving interaction with others of different racial, ethnic, and socioeconomic groups all may become sources of potential action based on a commitment to mankind. All of these activities must be considered a legitimate part of the curriculum and not viewed as extracurricular activities. A mankind curriculum will not be only a sedentary, isolated, intellectual exercise. It will include actions on behalf of mankind. Only by carrying out such actions can a student truly be said to possess a mankind perspective.

7. Subject matter in a mankind curriculum must be implemented in a supporting environment in all other aspects of the school.

Chapter 2 discussed the *Geist* of the school—the pervasive emotional climate—and Chapter 3 described the kind of human interaction that must occur in the classroom if students are to achieve an understanding of mankind and to develop a mankind perspective. Both of these aspects of schooling are essential in contributing to the impact of subject matter in a mankind curriculum. A free and open examination of a variety of perspectives, for example, cannot occur in a punitive, authoritative classroom or school environment under the direction of poorly educated teachers with few or no up-to-date curricular materials. It cannot occur unless the resources of the school are committed to making possible the exploration of topics from many perspectives.

Equally important are the processes involved in the curriculum and in instruction. The spirit of inquiry must be pervasive and characteristic of the way in which the teacher functions and the student pursues his learnings. Mistakes should be viewed as a natural part of learning and of man's behavior and not as failures. Learning skills such as research and communications skills and positive attitudes toward learning which will equip each student for lifelong learning are also an essential part of a mankind curriculum.

An understanding of mankind requires a wide array of resources. Instructional materials on many subjects with relevance to man and his conditions of living must be available for students to use. Primary sources must also be used, and the various interpretations of them must be analyzed. Resources from the broader community must be used if the richness of the diversity of man and his conditions of living are to be exemplified. Art studios and galleries, concerts, industries, businesses, museums, all need to be a part of the educative process. All of the preceding examples are believed to be a part of the kind of supportive environment needed to maximize the impact of subject matter in a mankind curriculum.

Subject matter alone cannot effectively achieve the goals of this proposed curriculum: understanding of the concept of mankind and the development of a mankind perspective. Mankind is not a static, unchanging concept but is dynamic and evolving. An understanding of man must be pursued with compatible processes and in a supportive environment.

Applying the Criteria to Subject Matter

As the traditional curriculum of most schools is examined in relation to the foregoing criteria, it becomes evident that some modifications and some major changes need to be made. Changes need to be made within the subject matter traditionally included in the curriculum and by the inclusion of new sources for subject matter.

In order to meet the criteria for subject matter in a mankind curriculum, all of the traditional subject areas would need some modification. However, because of the close relationship between the concept of mankind and the content of the social studies, this subject area would probably require considerable redirection. We have selected history for discussion here as an example of how the seven criteria can be applied to various facets of the curriculum.

To contribute to an understanding of the concept of mankind, the study of history should clearly point to the common human attributes that all historical leaders have possessed: values, emotions, needs, thought, and ability to communicate. Particular study might be made of those leaders who have personified the mankind assumptions—the kinds of values a person with a mankind perspective would hold about his fellow man. Examples of such persons might be Gandhi and Martin Luther King. Primary sources about these men could be contemporary newspaper and magazine articles. Biographies could be read and events in which they figured studied.

If history is to be in agreement with and is to support the concept of mankind and a mankind perspective, a much greater increase is needed in the scope of the content. Mankind includes all people, not only those groups who live in the Western world. History would need to become a more global subject with much more attention given to the non-Western world. The history of Africa and Japan must be studied, for example, before the interests of Westerners reached these countries. History must be the study of the significant contributions of all people to the advancement of civilization.

If history is to have relevance to mankind, it must always present the diversity of man in a positive way, never as the history of one group of people as superior to another group. Engle suggests that the persistent problems of mankind must become a focus of study.[8]

History can also help meet the fourth criterion for subject matter in a mankind curriculum. Knowledge of differing groups of people, their historical development, their problems, and their successes can contribute to the student's ability to understand himself and to transcend himself.

To help the student examine topics from many perspectives, historical and current issues must be included in the curriculum which lend themselves to this procedure. Examples of some possibilities are:

1. An examination of man's rights and freedom in today's world and the search for these according to the Western interpretation, the communistic interpretation, and a South African interpretation (from both blacks and whites).
2. The resolution of conflict. The avenues open to man, the advantages and disadvantages of each avenue, and the identification of those most in keeping with the mankind ideal.
3. A consideration of the American Revolutionary War from both the American and British interpretations.

If history is to promote action based on a commitment to mankind, students should be provided with outlets for action on current issues on behalf of mankind which are appropriate to their developmental level. Peaceful protests about war, a barrage of letters to government officials about discrimination, or a demonstration of a variety of ways by which men can and have resolved conflict might be actions showing a beginning commitment to mankind at various developmental levels of students in history classes.

Finally, history must be taught in a supportive environment. Issues, knowledge, actions, values, attitudes, and opinions must be developed in an inquiry mode of learning with the teacher serving as a resource and guide to learning, rather than as the "fount of wisdom." An array of all types of resources, both physical and human, must be made available to the student as he needs them. Primary sources, texts, and all types of multimedia materials will contribute to more effective learning in a mankind curriculum. The teacher must act in accordance with a concern for mankind, and especially for students, in an atmosphere of warm support. The purposes of the school must be mankind purposes, the organization of the school must be an open one which supports the search for a mankind perspective, and the leadership of the school must function with a mankind commitment toward the teachers and students.

These, then, are some ways in which history as a subject area might be modified to meet more closely the criteria for a mankind curriculum. All other subject areas in the traditional curriculum must be reconsidered in a similar way if a mankind curriculum is to be implemented.

More general examples are offered here also to suggest how other traditional content areas could be brought into closer agreement with the mankind idea. In physics, the concept of energy could be a topic of study which would include a consideration of the need all men have for energy, the types commonly available to various parts of the world, the gaps created by the limited availability of various forms of energy, and the problems and benefits man experiences as his forms of energy are utilized and changed. The inclusion of such topics would help bring science to a closer relevance to mankind and would be in agreement with and support the concept of mankind.

Literature could contribute to a greater understanding of mankind and to the development of a mankind perspective and have greater relevance to mankind through a study of selected works which are thought to be representative of the best of man's efforts to express himself in written form—no matter where or when the author may have lived. In addition to traditional readings found in American schools, a balanced program would include works by Gandhi, Confucius, Lao-tzu, Mishima, Tagore, and Markandaya as well as folktales from around the world. Similarly, art and music would include a study of all the major ways in which men have expressed their thoughts and feelings—not just music, paintings, and sculpture from the Renaissance through today from the Western countries. Civics offers many issues which can be examined from differing perspectives and which allow for appropriate action based on a commitment to mankind. Volunteering to work for political parties, attending city council meetings, collecting signatures for petitions, and helping get people out to vote are examples. Geography could be brought into a closer agreement with the concept of mankind by a consideration of how natural resources can be made more equally available to all men. Mathematics can contribute to a greater understanding of mankind by considering the number and measurement systems used by various groups with the advantages and the disadvantages of each in a technological world made explicit.

Perhaps not all of the criteria can be applied to each of the traditional subject areas with equal weight or intensity, but all areas must undergo a close scrutiny in relation to each of the criteria.

Contributions from Behavioral and Social Sciences: New Sources for the Curriculum

As the potential contributions of the traditional subject areas are examined in relation to the seven criteria, it becomes apparent that these subjects need to be supplemented by some that have man himself as the object of study: the behavioral sciences and other social sciences. As in the other group of subject areas, not all the criteria probably will be applied with equal weight to each of the disciplines.

Sady has identified three major themes of *anthropology:* the understanding of the biological unity of man, the existence of cultural diversity within a common human pattern, and the universality of the process of cultural change.[10] These themes fit well with the criteria we have identified for the inclusion of subject matter in a mankind curriculum, and, therefore, topics within anthropology can contribute to meeting many of these criteria. Knowledge and appreciation of a variety of cultures can assist in developing an understanding of the concept of mankind and can help the student to transcend his own culture. Child-rearing patterns, cultural values, differing forms of family life and family organization (the patriarchal family, the matriarchal family, the extended family, etc.), and patterns of social organization can be studied. Also, consideration of minority groups and how they live—their present needs, resources, and problems and attempts to solve them—should provide many outlets for action based on a commitment to mankind. For example, students can help clean up slums, can tutor disadvantaged children, and can help unrepresented minorities register to vote.

Psychology can contribute greatly to the first essential step in self-transcendence, insight into self and the development of a healthy ego. These two attributes enable a person to reach out to others—to transcend himself.

Social psychology and *sociology* can also contribute to a mankind curriculum. The understanding that man is a social animal with social needs and the study of human interaction are potential topics from social psychology that would contribute to an understanding of mankind and to the ability to transcend self. Instructional materials dealing with human relationships are now available on the commercial market. *The Intergroup Relations Curriculum*[11] and *First Things,* a multimedia program,[12] are examples at the elementary school level. Other topics include the effects of groups on man's life, the reasons that groups form, the effects of groups on members, the relationships among group members and among other groups, and a study of the problems of man.[13]

Ethics, in being concerned with standards of conduct among people in a social group,[14] can contribute to meeting some of the criteria. Students can be helped to develop skills in analyzing actions according to specified standards to be sure that actions which they take to express a commitment to mankind are helpful and not harmful to mankind. An action to help one group of people which harms another group, for example, is not in agreement with the concept of mankind. Ethics can also assist in the understanding of the concept of mankind through analyses of how mankind assumptions operate as standards of conduct.

Ecology, viewed in part as man's behavior in relation to his environment, can help to meet some of the criteria. Actions based on a commitment to mankind can have many outlets in this subject area. Identifying and assisting to correct sources of pollution, writing letters to government officials supporting or condemning various construction projects (after serious study of the issues, of course), cleaning up a river or lake within the community, collecting materials for recycling, and even simply keeping the campus clean are possibilities. There are also many issues within ecology which can be examined from differing perspectives.

The view represented in this brief discussion of a mankind curriculum is, of necessity, broad. A few subject areas cannot adequately meet all of the criteria suggested for subject matter; a wide array of subject areas is needed. The examples which we have discussed of modifications needed in subject matter have been based on the currently popular discipline-centered curriculum. Even should this approach change during the next decade or so, the substance of the curriculum—whether it be organized as integrated broad fields of studies, or as problems, or as the concerns of the learner and society—must still be evaluated by these criteria if a mankind curriculum is to be implemented.

The role of the disciplines as viewed here is somewhat different than has been popular in the past. The subject matter is not included to exemplify the structure of the discipline as it was during the curriculum reform efforts of the 1960s, although it might continue to contribute to this. Rather, subject matter is included primarily because of its contribution to the understanding of mankind and the development of a mankind perspective. The role of subject matter thus becomes a means toward an end rather than an end in itself.

It is recognized that a curriculum has other goals to achieve: development of communication skills, responsible citizenship, self-actualization, and other often-quoted goals still remain. But these goals must be overarched by the goal of an understanding of mankind and the development of a mankind perspective. Traditional goals need not be eliminated in a mankind curriculum; indeed, most goals which have been considered significant in the past probably make a contribution to the mankind perspective.

The implementation of a mankind curriculum will be facilitated by several curricular trends already in existence today. Organizing the social studies curriculum around social issues and problems, including values as a legitimate curricular topic; inquiry-oriented learning materials; the study of differing cultural areas and minority groups; and an ever-broadening array of learning materials available for student use are very promising trends in the social studies which will make that subject area at least more compatible with a mankind curriculum. In addition, the humanistic concern for the development of the individual, including self-understanding; the availability of an overwhelming array of learning materials in an ever-expanding array of curricular topics; and the emphasis upon skills to facilitate lifelong learning are other trends already being implemented which would also be compatible with a mankind curriculum.

We believe that implementing a mankind curriculum is not "pie-in-the-sky" but a very feasible possibility not too far removed from what might be considered as a "good" education today. The mankind perspective as developed through a mankind curriculum is an urgently needed attribute of all people in the world today. It must be fostered by all institutions concerned with education and particularly the schools.

Notes

1. Robert Ulrich (ed.), *Education and the Idea of Mankind,* Harcourt, Brace & World, Inc., New York, 1964, p 27.

2. Harold C. Wells with John T. Canfield, *About Me,* student book and teacher guide, Encyclopedia Britannica Educational Corporation, Chicago, 1971.

3. *Moods and Emotions,* a set of study prints, Child's World, Inc., Mankato, Minn. 56001, 1969.

4. *Learning about Me,* Q-ED Productions, 2921 West Alameda Avenue, Burbank, Calif. 91505.

5. *What Is Prejudice?* Warren Schloat Productions, Inc., Pleasantville, N.Y. 10570.

6. *From Subject to Citizen,* developed by the Educational Development Center and distributed by Denoyer-Geppert, 5235 Ravenswood Avenue, Chicago 60640, 1970.

7. *Opposing Viewpoints Library,* Glenhaven Press, Box 831, Anoka, Minn. 55303.

8. Shirley H. Engle, "World History Based on the Problems of Mankind," *The Indiana Social Studies Quarterly,* vol. 17, Autumn 1964.

9. A number of publications give broad directions or specific suggestions about how particular subject areas might be revised to come in closer agreement with the concept of mankind. Although these suggestions are not made with any reference to the criteria stated in this chapter, they might be valuable resources to the reader. See, for example, Elliot W. Eisner, "Education and the Idea of Mankind," mimeographed paper, Council for the Study of Mankind, no date; John I. Goodlad, "The Objectives of American Education and the Interdependent World," *The Indiana Social Studies Quarterly,* vol. 18, Winter 1965-1966, pp. 8-16; and Gerhard Hirschfeld, "Teachers Should Understand Mankind," *Teachers College Record,* vol. 70, March 1969, pp. 541-548.

10. Rachel Reese Sady, "Anthropology and the Idea of Mankind," mimeographed paper, Council for the Study of Mankind, no date.

11. John S. Gibson, *The Intergroup Relations Curriculum,* Lincoln-Filene Center for Citizenship and Public Affairs, Tufts University, Medford, Mass., 1969.

12. *First Things: Sound Filmstrips for Primary Years,* Guidance Associates, Pleasantville, N.Y. 10570, 1970.

13. The ideas included here which sociology may contribute are adapted from Caroline B. Rose, *Sociology,* Charles E. Merrill Books, Inc., Columbus, Ohio, 1965.

14. "Ethics," *International Encyclopedia of the Social Sciences,* The Free Press, New York, 1968, pp. 160-167.

Chapter 5
Emergence of a Mankind Curriculum: The Teachers Plan

This chapter describes the planning of a mankind curriculum for children by a group of five teachers who have together compiled this account. Intense interest, complete involvement, wholehearted commitment, high elation, and headlong productivity together with false starts, blind alleys, discouragement, and nonproductivity characterized our work and spirit. It is not the purpose of this chapter to provide a history of our deliberations and work processes over a period of eighteen months, the ideas explored and discarded, the roles played by the various members, and the like. Our purpose, instead, is to present the essence of the deliberations, a synthesis of the thinking and decisions of the group. In short, what appears here represents the state of a proposed mankind curriculum as it stood a few days before the actual beginning of an experimental summer session for children—bone and sinew with a little flesh and no fat at all.

Curriculum Planning

It will be useful first, however, to comment briefly on some pertinent prior experiences of the members of the planning group and the appropriateness of the University Elementary School at UCLA as the setting for the proposed experiment. During the previous decade, the faculty of the University Elementary School (UES) had worked on developing goals for the total school as well as more specific outcomes for each of the four phases of elementary schooling: early childhood, lower elementary, middle elementary, and upper elementary. Originating with the early childhood phase and continuing throughout the elementary school years, major concern was that the individual child know and accept himself—his feelings, strengths, and weaknesses—and view himself as a person of worth. Following closely in importance was the focus on his relationships to other children and to teachers. Groups of teachers had worked together in describing specific behaviors which were thought to exemplify the general goals in these areas. Many strategies were attempted in seeking to promote achievement of these sometimes elusive objectives. Some were effective and some were not. In the process, however, the groups of teachers learned to work together on the tasks of stating, refining, clarifying, defending, and teaching toward objectives, followed by revising them in the light of this process.

Clearly, the UES staff as a whole had been at work designing a curriculum for children which emphasized many objectives directly or indirectly related to mankind concepts. Central and overarching in this curriculum was the concern for learners to achieve self-knowledge and self-acceptance. Closely related were objectives for self-regulating and self-propelling behaviors. In addition, the entire staff had planned and implemented learning experiences for children, ages four through twelve, in some of man's currently unsolved problems such as poverty and pollution, in affective behavior, in developing a perspective toward the social and physical world, and in decision making. The fact that the faculty had spent a considerable amount of time in defining, describing, planning, and teaching toward these goals provided us with a great deal of knowledge about what was probable and what was possible with respect to achievement, as well as productive means to these ends.

We five UES teachers who were invited to plan the segment of curriculum for children for the experimental summer sessions, then, not only were widely experienced teachers but also had participated, to some degree and for varying lengths of time, in curriculum committee work with a humanistic orientation. We centered our work on the blending of two documents. The first document had its origin in one of the routine total staff meetings held regularly at UES. At that meeting, John Goodlad, at that time Director of UES, who was already deeply involved with the Council for the Study of Mankind, Inc., proposed five values:

1. Each human life is of inestimable significance. Each phase of human life is as important and significant as any other phase of human life.
2. Human immortality depends on the ability of human beings to transcend themselves and truly identify with others—their needs, their interests, their destiny, their humanness.
3. The proper study for man is mankind.
4. Understanding man depends on viewing his existence from a mankind perspective.
5. What learners do in the pursuit of knowledge has value in itself quite apart from the ends, outcomes, or accomplishments of that pursuit. There is more, then, to curriculum, teaching, and evaluation than preoccupation with goals.

The second document reflects the then current, but always evolving, statement of objectives held for children at the University Elementary School. A few examples of these objectives are given here.

Some objectives in the areas of self-control, self-reliance, self-appraisal, self-release, decision making, and ability to deal with and adapt to change are:

1. predicts effects and consequences of his behavior
2. evaluates his own performance and expresses satisfaction with realistic achievement
3. identifies his problems
4. makes decisions from available alternatives

In the area of personal relations with adults, peers, groups, and authority:

1. can seek or accept needed guidance and support from an adult

2. accepts similarities and differences among peers; assists others in the pursuit of valid goals
3. contributes to group decision making

Among the objectives stated for aesthetic development through the visual arts are:

1. shows by his behavior an awareness of individuality of the art products of self and others both by his performance in studio experiences and by verbal evaluation of artists' works
2. understands that the visual elements (line, shape, texture, color, etc.) are universal and available to all men

The UES statement of objectives also includes content and pedagogical criteria for selecting learning opportunities for particular groups of learners in a humanistic curriculum. According to these criteria, content must:

1. be related to a study of contemporary mankind
2. have transfer value to humanistic aims
3. buttress and support learning in other fields
4. have unresolved issues
5. have generalizability
6. focus on the uniqueness of individuals
7. focus on the interrelatedness of the individual, his group, and his society
8. have a high possibility for the student to take an assumed position or viewpoint
9. be related to the child's own life
10. have significance in its own right
11. encourage student practice of behavior sought
12. contribute to simultaneous objectives listed under self and interpersonal relations
13. build on what has gone before and prepare for what is to come
14. be comprehensive in that it includes several ideas and catch-hold points for differing student interests

The pedagogical criteria are:

1. encompass ability levels of the group

2. build on what has gone before and prepare for what is to come
3. have continuity and sequence
4. be comprehensive in that they include several ideas and catch-hold points for differing student interests
5. tie together students, ideas, and materials in some meaningful fashion
6. be part of the child's world and be relevant to his experiences
7. have high interest level for children
8. provide firsthand experiences (i.e., provide for physical and emotional involvement)
9. encourage formulation of further hypotheses
10. provide opportunity for children to work together in groups of various sizes[1]

This, then, was our level of thinking and development at the beginning of the project with respect to general guidelines for effective curriculum planning.

Planning the Mankind Curriculum

When we were invited to participate in the mankind project, all five of us were tremendously excited and stimulated by the ideas and aspirations inherent in the project. Not one of us even momentarily considered declining the invitation to become involved on behalf of children. Not one of us hesitated to commit to the project a major portion of our personal time for the coming eighteen months. Each of us, at that point, was more intrigued than disturbed by the openness, ambiguities, and potential of the project.

We found it to be more productive to concentrate our meeting time in large blocks rather than to hold many relatively short, after-school conferences. Several hours on Friday afternoon followed by an all-day session on Saturday was the usual pattern over the eighteen-month period, plus a series of successive whole days in the summer. Between these meetings, there was a time for background reading, assigned tasks, and reflection.

In the early meetings, a major portion of the time was needed for clarifying an understanding of mankind assumptions, commonplaces of man, mankind perspective, and other concepts, a process which still goes on. In our deliberations, we selected from the list of mankind assumptions (presented in Chapter 4) those which we felt would hold the most meaning for children of elementary school age. Then we generated many learning opportunities that might lead to that particular value while meeting the content and pedagogical criteria already mentioned. All of us, though perhaps most insistently the three members who were to teach the summer session for children,[2] felt that a rigidity of expectation and learning experiences was to be diligently avoided. Greatest flexibility was to be maintained since preconceived objectives and experiences might prove to be inappropriate for the volunteering student population. Instead, general directions were thoroughly explored, described, and decided upon. Many learning experiences were discussed and categorized. During the summer session the teachers were to have maximum freedom in their day-to-day planning to choose those directions and those experiences that were, in their judgment, appropriate for the particular group of learners.

The most constantly recurring themes during the eighteen months of intermittent discussion included some of the criteria mentioned earlier and provided additional ones. It was decided, for example, that the activity selected for or by children should:

1. be sufficiently intense to create tension leading to conflict, which then must be resolved in some manner other than withdrawal
2. require maximum interaction of the learners
3. have obvious natural consequences rather than arbitrary consequences imposed by the teacher
4. demand emotional as well as physical involvement
5. *not* be an abstract intellectual exercise but instead deal with problems that are real to the child
6. reveal values
7. promote divergent thinking
8. provide alternatives for choice
9. provide a goal for students so attractive that conflicts would be subordinate to the attainment of that goal through group effort and interdependence of children
10. provide maximum experience away from the school base
11. be significantly different from usual school procedures and not solely the cognitive three R's approach

Some examples of activities that meet some or all of these criteria are provided later in this chapter.

These criteria are applicable to all ages. Consequently, our planning group had to seek other bases for deciding on the ages of children to be included in the summer session. The ages of nine to twelve were chosen for three reasons. First, although younger ages present the opportunity of reaching children before characteristic behavior has been firmly established—we were very conscious of the data on early learning—we were faced with the problem of limited materials for the young. Directly related to this, we did not wish to add to our manifold problems the additional problem of teaching basic language skills. Second, older children are accustomed to school, thus removing the problem of using a substantial portion of the very short summer session for orienting younger children to school life. And finally, we wanted to see which problems of unfulfilled self-transcendence still remained with these older children as we sought to move them toward the mankind vision.

Another early discussion in our planning group pertained to the adult-child ratio. Differentiated staffing and team teaching are long-established practices at the University Elementary School, but they are not in most schools. These modified staffing patterns do not necessarily cost more; in fact they can cost less than the conventional self-contained classroom. But they add many benefits, we think, especially in making possible, usually, a higher ratio of adults to children. This benefit appears to be of particular importance for the purposes we were seeking to achieve. For example, it brings teacher modeling of desired behavior closer to each child than is possible in the usual one-teacher classroom. Also, it requires that children interact with several quite different adults and, as well, gives them insights into aspects of role differentiation and division of labor. Such social attributes become potential objects of study.

We decided not to abandon our beliefs in and common practices of differentiative staffing, resulting in a higher ratio of adults to children, simply for the sake of making the project more like practices in most schools. School personnel must not continue to reject new ways simply because they do not fit readily with established patterns of school organization. These, too, can and should be changed if this is what is necessary for the adoption of innovations. We decided, therefore, on a 10 to 1 ratio of children to teachers, realizing full well that all of our adults were fully qualified and extensively experienced teachers, whereas differentiated staffing usually calls for increasing the ratio of adults to children by including aides, interns, clerks, parent volunteers, and the like.

We needed fully qualified personnel for other reasons. This was an experimental project. The conceptual framework guiding it was complex, abstract, and difficult for us all. The subject matter for the children was new to us. And we wanted to observe the children most carefully as we proceeded in order to determine strengths and weaknesses to be accounted for in seeking to translate and transmit our experience to others.

Narrowing the Focus

The mankind assumptions are complex, difficult to grasp at first, and even more difficult to relate to meaningful programs for children. As we read about and discussed mankind assumptions, it became clear that we would need to limit the focus of our deliberations. We decided to start with assumption 6 (in Chapter 4), "Mankind conditions and values take precedence over personal desires, ambitions, and values," and restate it in such a way that it could be operationalized. In other words, it became necessary to describe those behaviors that would characterize an individual who acted in accordance with this mankind assumption.

We first worked out the sequence of development the child goes through in reaching this point: The individual who has self-esteem, self-knowledge, and self-acceptance will be secure and comfortable enough to be reasonably free from anxiety and threat. Such a person can transcend his own immediate concerns and put himself in the place of another. This allows him to subordinate his own desires when that is necessary for the good or higher values of a group with which he is affiliated. This in turn will allow him to deal intellectually with the possibility of identifying with a remote or supraordinate group—mankind. We felt that in order to keep the program from becoming just another exercise in intellectualizing and verbalizing a value position, it was very important for us to see *process* as a dominant factor of equal importance to ends or goals and to focus our attention on moving the child through a sequence of development rather than concentrating only on the end we wanted to achieve.

Functioning always within the total framework described in the preceding chapters, the three main thrusts of the curriculum for children would be: (1) transcendence of segmental values, (2) interpersonal relations, and (3) man as a subject of study. The first thrust can be thought of as including the other two. It came to us in a flash of insight midway in our deliberations that the concept of transcendence is *the key* to a mankind perspective. The degree of emphasis on each of these strands could not be predicted in advance, since the characterisitics of the learners were unknown. Furthermore, on any sequence in each of the three areas, neither the entering behavior nor the terminal behavior at the end of six weeks of each learner could be predicted.

The kinds of interpersonal relations that we hoped to establish were dealt with in detail in Chapter 3, so that further discussion is redundant here, except to say that the planning group underestimated, or took for granted, the importance of intrapersonal and interpersonal relations as imperative prerequisites to cultural transcendence. The other two strands need amplification. "Transcends segmental values" is a restatement, in behavioral terms, of assumption 6: "Mankind conditions and values take precedence over personal desires, ambitions, and values." This statement was further detailed as follows:

1. recognizes own personal and social values and limits behaviors to those congruent with values of the group
2. accepts limitations, present state of development, and potentialities of self and others
3. allows others to hold differing values until there is conflict with an overarching set of values
4. accepts, enjoys, welcomes, values, and seeks the diversity of mankind

Each of these statements, then, was further expanded in ever greater detail and explicitness. For example, for the first, "recognizes own personal and social values and limits behavior to those congruent with values of the group," items such as the following were listed: uses the word *value;* defines the word *value;* distinguishes between a value and a fact and/or truth; separates learned and innate behavior; realizes how one gains or changes values; perceives how values are reflected in behavior; identifies own values and those of other individuals and groups; accepts or rejects values; joins a group and accepts its values; joins a group but doesn't accept its values and attempts to effect change; operates in and contributes to more than one group; and so on.

"Man as a subject of study," the third potential thrust of the curriculum for children, draws its content principally from the commonplaces of man cited in Chapter 4 ("All people value, all people have emotions, all people have needs, all people think, all people communicate") and from anthropology. This thrust is intimately and inextricably related to the fourth behavior listed under "transcends segmental values,"—"accepts, enjoys, welcomes, values, and seeks the diversity of mankind." We received invaluable help from Thomas LaBelle of the UCLA faculty in understanding the concepts and processes of the anthropologist. We intended to use these at the child's level if it turned out to be appropriate. The children would observe behaviors, expectations, and values in themselves as well as in other individuals and groups. They would create their own system of categories such as family, education, work, and art, comparing and contrasting the specific items. Through this process, presumably, the learner would become aware of the commonality of human needs; the diversity in meeting human needs; the similarities within human experience; and the effect of one's culture on one's attitudes, values, language patterns, and ways of learning and thinking. The learner would also attempt to avoid assigning his own values to others as if they were fact or universal.

Some Alternatives Emerge

Next we identified the most promising *types* of activities for the purposes and objectives of the summer session. The list turned out to be extensive: trips and excursions of various lengths, kinds, purposes, and duration; interviews and observation of other individuals and groups; discussion groups of varying types, sizes, and duration; role playing, puppets, and masked drama; construction and other projects, both group and individual, perhaps with others as beneficiary; group games, stories, films, slides, posters, and videotapes of selves as material for observation and analysis; interest surveys and attitude scales; parties; commercial games that reveal values; programs for others, possibly parents or invalids; "live-ins" at school; and art and drama activities as an expression of values. The reader will note that these types of activities readily meet the content and pedagogical criteria given earlier.

In brainstorming the possible experiences and activities for the summer session, vividness and intensity were the overriding criteria. The first plan to be considered, and very reluctantly abandoned because of inadequate financial resources, was an extended study tour of various areas of California with the dual objective of close, round-the-clock interaction among the participants and teachers and observation of "cultural pockets" throughout the state (LaBelle, an anthropologist, had told us that there were seventeen such "pockets" in the Fresno area alone!). Another plan, that of being involved for a period of time in the daily activities of a contrasting culture, such as an Indian reservation, proved to be unfeasible. It could not be known at the time of proliferating alternatives that the highlight of the summer session would turn out to be a weekend in San Diego, which is described fully in the following chapter.

It was our intention to create awareness of and generate many more possible experiences than could be carried out in the short time available. With quantity and variety, the teachers of the session could then select those that seemed most appropriate once the learners presented themselves. It was never the plan to use all of them. The list of activities we finally compiled is far too extensive to be included here in its totality, but the examples given will indicate the scope of our thinking. We found it useful to categorize the learning experiences by using the three words *transcends, segmental,* and *values* as headings.

Transcends

Make a book "About Me."[3]

Identify and meet needs of other children.

Do something for another person or group.

Plan and take trips—insist on consensus with respect to destination and means, or "no go."

Organize available space for own work (from deliberate chaos).

Set up rules for resolving conflict.

Create a set of mankind values and compare with those of scholars.

Stay overnight at school.

Play a game for which two groups have been taught different rules.

Guide and communicate (verbally, nonverbally) with a blindfolded person.

Solve common problems.

Observe adults as they role-play conflict situations.

Generate and practice alternate ways to solve conflict; e.g., refer to mankind values, reach consensus, vote, flip a coin, have a contest, create a set of overarching rules or values.

Segmental

Study Mr. "O."[4]

Visit other schools, preferably ethnically or culturally different; observe values, interact, invite for return visit(s); make and compare family trees.

Engage in synectics (creative, imaginative thinking as an aid in problem solving).

Invite foreign students from the university campus to the classroom in order to interview them or to have them help children live in class according to family or cultural values.

Chart values, behaviors, and expectations, developing categories (universals) and comparing diversities.

Study what a child of similar age does in another culture.

Compare two cultures, not including one's own.

Plan a school for the children of a particular culture.

Values

Study values per se: define, use word, identify, discriminate between value and nonvalue statements, etc.

Develop an artificial value system and live by it.

Create utopia—the perfect school, classroom, family, community, etc.—and express it through art, model, story, poem, written description, or other media.

Interview another in class.

Make predictions based on a set of values.

Observe behavior and identify values represented.

Given a set of values, tell end of a story.

Create a planet on which live groups with conflicting values.

Some of these activities were incorporated into the summer program, some were found to be inappropriate, and for others there was no time. The following chapter discusses the program in detail as it developed over the six-week session and concludes with retrospective comments of students and teachers.

Notes

1. The lists of content and pedagogical criteria were adapted and then expanded from John I. Goodlad, "The Teacher Selects, Plans, and Organizes," *Learning and the Teacher,* 1959 Yearbook of the Association for Supervision and Curriculum Development, Washington, D.C., 1959, pp.39-60.

2. Roxie Lee, Kent Lewis, Douglas O. Russell.

3. Harold C. Wells and John T. Canfield, *About Me,* Combined Motivation Systems, Inc., 630 River Road, Rosemont, Ill.. 1971.

4. Science Curriculum Improvement Study, *Unit on "Relativity,"* D. C. Heath and Company, Boston, 1968.

Chapter 6

A Mankind School in Action:
An Observer's Report

The preceding chapter demonstrates our belief in careful planning for teaching and learning. Such planning is based, necessarily, on general knowledge about learners and their home environments and what will be appropriate for the age group. It must be conducted with the full realization that its fruits often will not be appropriate for specific individuals and must be discarded in favor of other alternatives. But even the new alternatives must be considered in the light of the larger goals and concepts guiding the total program. They provide a framework for decision making in the same way that certain architectural concepts provide a framework within which the architect seeks to work as he designs a house for his clients.

This chapter describes, more or less chronologically, the events of the six-week summer session that was the product of eighteen months of planning. It will be seen how initial plans had to be revised daily and sometimes hourly in the light of new evidence, how the children entered into the process, and how earlier planning paid off in assisting the teachers both to be flexible on one hand and to be firm on the other, especially in insisting that the children assume responsibility for their own acts and the consequences of those acts.

Three of the initial group of five teachers taught the children. We make no apologies for the fact that these teachers possess first-rate teaching ability. Not only are they experienced and well prepared, but, in addition, they have taught in teams for years and are not neophytes with respect to concepts of humanistic education. We feel it is important to stress the need for teachers to know what they are about when they venture into new realms. Too many good curricular and pedagogical ideas have been discredited simply because the teachers involved were not prepared adequately to do justice to them.

The summer group of children consisted of 14 boys and 10 girls ranging in age from 9 to 13, most of them being 10 or 11. Five of the children were black and two were of Japanese extraction. Regrettably, the summer programs at UCLA must be self-sustaining, and our limited funds did not permit tuition scholarships. Consequently, the fee partially selected a higher socioeconomic level of children than we had hoped for.

During the first week a semistructured interview was conducted with each child in an attempt to determine the extent to which each tended to think beyond immediate self-interest. The most productive of the questions asked were: "Most of us have things we would like to have changed. What are some of the things you'd like to see different?" "Most of us have things we worry about from time to time. What are some of the things you worry about?" "What are some of the things you hope for?" "If you could have three wishes, what would they be?" "If you could give some message to all the people of the world, what would you tell them?"

Results showed a very wide range of concerns. For example, 10-year-old John D. describing what he would like to see changed said, "The end of pollution and war. People to be treated equally no matter what color they are. Schools with more ideas than just repeating the same things every day. And there should be fair politics—let voters decide." On the other hand, almost-10-year-old Lori said, "I'd like to see us get our old maid back—the one we have now is pregnant, and we're always having to do the things she ought to be doing... and I hope I have a nice birthday this year—all I got last year was one dress." Again, 11-year-old Caryn told what she would like to see changed: "Discrimination. Every person should have equal rights—an equal chance to prove what they can do. And we should have everyone doing something about ecology and pollution. To do it we must give up some of our advantages." Eleven-year-old Nikki hoped to get another raccoon and wished that the dew wouldn't get her feet wet in the early morning. Lynne, however, wished there were "more doctors and medical help in countries like Pakistan." George wished "to live in a great big giant house with a giant pool, to own three big hotels in New York, and to have billions of dollars"; Marc wanted "a new volleyball and a basketball and a handball." The three wishes question did not, however, elicit that kind of a personal-desire answer from all. Eleven-year-old Doug's wishes were to "stop pollution, everybody could find a decent place to live and enough food, and not having the government going out of control, getting power and then overusing it."

General Instructional Planning

From the results of these interviews and from what teachers observed, it was obvious that there were individual differences in identifying with mankind concerns, and it was apparent that a certain range and flexibility of program would be necessary. Therefore, a general framework was set up in the beginning, to be filled out as the class sessions progressed according to the needs and the limitations which emerged.

In working together to develop a curriculum with a mankind perspective, the teachers had tended to use interchangeably the terms "mankind curriculum" and "humanistic curriculum for children." For them, "humanistic" was described most accurately by the definition "marked by or expressive of devotion to human welfare or strong interest in or concern for man."[1] They had talked in terms of the humanistic child and the steps to be projected as necessary to bring a student to this state of humanism. Given these particular children, it became necessary to devise learning experiences which would move each one of them from where he was to a step further along the way. Focus on the three elements of values, diversity-similarity, and self-transcendence remained paramount, though the degree of emphasis and manner of focusing shifted somewhat from tentative earlier plans.

Before describing the actual activities carried out during this six-week program, let us review the general steps proposed by the teachers in seeking to move a child toward a mankind perspective. They believed that the first requisite was that a child have knowledge of self, an awareness of what he himself is like as a person. He would need to have some awareness, next, of the thoughts and feelings of another person close to him or of several close members of his immediate group. He would then move toward seeing his place in a larger group, mankind, of which he is one member.

These steps were projected as taking place, first, within the summer session classroom. Next would come movement to the outdoors, to expand the environment. In making group decisions about proposed trips and then in going on such excursions, children could seek to understand themselves as individuals and as members of a group. Yet another goal was to bring together these students with members of a group quite different from their own, to promote interaction skills, greater self-knowledge, and some beginnings of understanding of the behavior of people of another cultural background. And for further expansion of a mankind perspective, it was hoped that at least some children could begin, through literature, to come to some understanding of what it is to be another person of a very different background, living in a very different setting, and having his own unique problems to work out.

Learning Activities in the Classroom

And now to the activities of the summer. Classes were held from 9 until 12 five mornings a week. Generally, the first hour and a half was spent on learning activities planned by the teachers. During this period, children sometimes worked together in one large group, at other times in one of three small groups, and from time to time by themselves. The next half hour was Choice, a free time set up so that children could express their values by selecting one of a number of activities. The last hour was spent again on learning activities planned by teachers and last-minute cleaning up of the classroom areas. From time to time there were trips, exchange visits with another school, and finally an intensified living experience where children spent the weekend together in San Diego. The teachers spent considerable time in a team meeting after each session, discussing the events of the morning and planning some of the details for the following day's program.

The first few days saw an emphasis on getting acquainted. The three teachers started it out, each in turn, by telling the children some personal things about themselves: what they were like, what they enjoyed, what they disliked having to do, and so on. The tone was friendly, inviting the children to begin looking upon their teachers as human beings, not just as adult authorities. Looks on the faces of some of the children suggested that this was for them a puzzling turn of events—grown-ups sitting down on the floor with you and talking to you as friends!

Besides serving to set the tone for the summer, introducing themselves this way provided a means of modeling for the students what would be a continuing major project for them throughout the session: an "About Me" book or box. Each teacher had made up one about himself and demonstrated the kinds of things one could put into such a book or box which would tell many different and unique things about oneself: a family tree, a personal data sheet, a list of favorite things to do and places to go. Throughout the summer, as will be described as we go along, suggestions were made of interesting pages which could be added to the About Me books. This project provided what turned out to be a most effective way for a child to achieve the first step, that of self-knowledge.

After teachers had introduced themselves, getting acquainted continued as children and teachers sat in a circle on the floor and played the Name Game. In this game, someone starts and says his own name, and the person next to him says the first person's name and then his own; the third person says the names of the first and second persons and then his own. The game continues around the circle, with the last person having the task of calling out the names of every person in the circle. The children obviously enjoyed this game, their eyes lighting up when someone remembered and called off their names. Children who consistently forgot the names of one or two specific children were given the task of remembering these names the next day. Sometimes there were variations, such as saying one's name and adding a hobby or perhaps a descriptive adjective about oneself.

While this activity perhaps has a simpleminded ring to it, there is no question that it was a most effective first step in building up recognition of self as a member of a group and eventually in building up group cohesiveness. Children were encouraged to call each other by name, rather than "hey, you." That the learning of the names of others does not come easily was demonstrated when these children exchanged visits with children in another summer school program. The other children did not know each other's names in many cases. The UES children commented on this, and a number remarked at the end of the summer, "It was lots easier to make friends in this school than in my regular school."

Another early activity designed to encourage knowing oneself and others was having children pair up and interview each other for one minute. That pair then got together with another pair, and each child told this small group what he had learned about the person he had just interviewed.

The Blind Walk was another early and productive activity. Children paired up and one child pretended to be blind while the other child led him around the classroom and yard. No verbal communication was permitted, and so the "sighted" child had to think up ways of communicating to the "blind" on the kinds of obstacles that were coming up. Afterward, children were asked to explore their feelings about this experience, what it was like for them, what they noticed that their partner had done which made them feel safe, when they felt fear, what body movements of the other person gave them information, how they had communicated without speaking.

A first-day activity which not only encouraged thinking about "What I'm like" but also created the need for room organization was making a collage which "tells what you're like." Children were asked to look through magazines, find pictures which could tell something about themselves, and then cut these out and paste them on poster board. These would then be shared with each other at the group meeting as a further way of getting to learn about people in the class.

The two classrooms purposely had been left completely bare, with all the desks, chairs, bookcases, and so on stacked up in the corners. The children did not question this and simply went to work on the bare floor. When they had finished their collages and went to meet in their small groups, teachers could then ask, "What can we do with the furniture that's around? First, would you like a place of your own to work? If so, what would you like?" Here, as throughout the program, emphasis was on setting alternatives and making choices. At first some children were baffled: "At my school the desks are all set up in rows, and the teacher tells you 'Go sit there,' and you go sit there. You can't suggest anything different." Children were told, "Well, here it is different. You can set up what you want."

There followed an enthusiastic period of furniture moving and some interesting desk placements. Some children chose to set up their desks entirely apart from everyone else. Others chose to set their desks in front of one of the sofas and share the seating. Some elected to isolate their desks but share them with one other child. One cluster of desks was set up in which a number of children would work in close quarters, with desks arranged in such a way that children were almost boxed in together. In one case, two sets of children (two boys and two girls) had designs on the same area. Loud complaints ensued, and it was soon apparent that the children expected the teacher to come over and tell them who could have the space and who would have to give it up. Instead, the teacher came over and asked, "What alternatives can you think of to solve this?" At first this seemed beyond their imaginations, but as the teacher continued to suggest that they might be able to work it out, the children were able to come to a solution: by moving out a large cupboard of blocks there would be room for all four children in the area. With no further prompting, the boys, who had been ranting against the girls, took over the job of moving out the blocks and even went on to move the girls' desk in and lowered it to a height convenient for them.

Children made name labels for their desks and chairs, and their own unique arrangement of desks persisted until the end of the session.

They had chosen a working arrangement which was satisfying for themselves and others and were happy to live with their decisions.

During this time, discussion continued as to "What else can we do with the furniture and the other things that are around?" Children suggested a listening center with records they would bring from home; posters; and tables for a game center for checkers, Monopoly, and jigsaw puzzles. A reading center was suggested, with children to choose books from the library to fill the empty bookcases. Two more sofas were brought in to make this a cozier spot. These centers were then available to the children at Choice time.

It appeared to teachers that these children were not accustomed to having a variety of choices and were not at home with choosing. It was apparently safer for them to do something a teacher had set up. One boy in particular was lost when left on his own but could be quite productive when assigned a specific structured task. For him it marked considerable progress when, toward the end of the summer, he was able to ask several boys what they were going to do so that he could at least choose to the extent of deciding a *person* he wanted to work with.

Other Choice time activities included playing volleyball or basketball (some days), going to the library, talking with friends, doing carpentry, wrestling, working on About Me, or going to the woods or gully on the school grounds. As the children began making choices which were increasingly more productive for themselves, this time period was extended by fifteen minutes.

Because the Blind Walk had so successfully elicited talk about feelings, some other similar activities were introduced. The children, sitting around a circular table, closed their eyes and stretched their hands out, palms upward. The teacher designated one of them to go around the table touching the palms of each child, and then everyone tried to guess who it was that had touched their hands. Two further exercises were found productive of knowing and trusting: levitation, in which two or more people pick up another person and lift him up high, and an exercise where one child closes his eyes and leans all the way to one side and then the other, with a person on either side to break his fall.

The obvious success of these activities led teachers next to introduce wrestling outside on a tumbling mat in the woods. Rules were set up to ensure fairness and safety, and wrestling became one of the most popular activities from then on. At first, wrestlers were mostly a few athletic boys, but eventually girls started wrestling each other, and finally even a few mixed wrestling matches were seen. For one girl, watching the wrestling marked the first time she had joined anyone else in an activity group or had even smiled. Wrestling, then, for both those who participated and those who watched, was a good friendship promoter.

Work was started during the first week on About Me books and continued throughout the session, sometimes as an assigned job, sometimes by a student's choice. First pages included a personal data sheet, a family tree, and fingerprints of self and some friends. Next added were sheets on "If I were..." (a bird, a flower, an animal, a car, etc.) and "This is me" ("I am happiest when..., I get angry when..., I am frightened by..., I feel love when..., I put trust in..., I feel hurt when...," etc.). Next, children discussed in their small groups "I am a success when...," and then went to work writing about it. A success chart was added for children to fill in with their most important successes at various age levels and the reasons they were experienced as successful. The chart concluded with successes hoped for within the next two years. A teacher showed how she had added some snapshots to her About Me book, and many children chose to bring pictures from home to add to their own books. Children were asked to work on "If I were a learning place...," and told they might do pictures with explanatory notes, write a story or poem, or choose their own way of describing an ideal learning place. They were thus led to think about what kinds of situations were conducive to learning for them personally and what sorts of things they would like to learn about. Children discussed in the small groups some of the important things they had learned out of school and in school and then went on to write these up for their book, ranking the things learned in order of their importance for them. A diary of the visits to another school was added, as well as a page on "How I spend my money and how I'd *like* to spend my money." An autograph page was added toward the end.

Children worked on this project with varying degrees of interest. Some got past very little more than date and place of birth and perhaps their fingerprints without prompting. They were encouraged to do at least some work on their books during the time planned for such work, and toward the end teachers helped those children who had done little to finish up what they wanted to take home. Other children needed no urging and worked enthusiastically on their books. Adrianne traced her family tree back to the eighteenth century and pasted up family photographs going back seventy years. Dave wrote a list of two hundred things he had learned outside of school. He also included a story he had written at his regular school and his regular school yearbook, as well as pictures of himself when he was much younger. He told a teacher that he had always thought of himself as an ugly person but that as he worked on his book he began to realize that might not be so. (Dave was tall for his age, had low self-esteem, and signed people's autograph pages "The Giant Dwarf.") Amanda showed an interesting example of movement ahead. The first day for her collage on "What I'm like" she had covered her poster with huge orange block letters proclaiming ME, AMANDA!! The end of the summer saw her getting a new folder for her About Me book and leaving the front cover blank. She wrote, "I'm not me. Sometimes I'm many people. I'm sick of everybody titling their folder ME. My book has no title." One might suggest that Amanda had begun to recognize that there is a good deal more to the world than just herself.

Introducing Mankind Ideas

Teachers early introduced another project which they hoped would serve as the beginning of a mankind framework. In the large group children were asked to list some of the rules that applied to everyone in their regular schools. This was then extended to the city, the state, and the nation. Their job in the small groups, they were told, would be for each one of them to think up five rules which everyone in the world could live by.

The rules suggested varied widely. Marc wrote, "Do not talk out of turn; you cannot undress." Paul said, "You must eat by 8 P.M., curfew will be at midnight, and ladies must not work more than six hours." Kelly's list cautioned, "Be peaceful; kill people who fight." Cornell added, "No cracking safes for practice." On the other hand, John O.'s list included, "Everyone can live without enemies; it doesn't matter what color they come in, they're all the same; everyone can live without violence, and everyone can improve." Laura added, "Communicate with everyone," and Amanda wrote, "People should care about their community and the people that live in it."

After the children had written up their rules, each, was paired with another child and the two of them were asked to combine their ideas into just five rules. They had to reach consensus; that is, both had to agree on each of the five rules. If a rule came up which one or the other could not accept, that rule was to be discarded and another thought up which would be acceptable for both. It was pointed out that this was another way of coming to decisions—by consensus rather than by voting.

For some, this exercise no doubt initiated thinking about a mankind world. It was useful for all, however, for it gave children a chance to work together and learn what another person thought and to learn about thinking of alternatives, coming to an agreement, and deciding. It also gave an opportunity for teachers to point out, as they continued to do from time to time, that "it's easy enough to make rules, but not so easy to keep them. Does everyday behavior match what people say the world should live by?"

While all these activities designed for knowing self and others were going on, attention was also being given to group experiences. Throughout, children met in one large group for certain discussion and planning activities and broke up into three small groups for other activities. Emphasis in the small groups was on developing listening, speaking, and interaction skills. For both the large and small groups, there was to be continuing emphasis on two things: look at what you are doing and then at what you say you are doing; and, there are alternatives for you in almost any situation—very often you can choose for yourself, after you've thought about the consequences of your choice.

The first day, children were asked to place themselves into three groups of eight. What happened might have been anticipated, although it had not been: two of the groups were made up entirely of boys, the third entirely of girls. (This reluctance of the sexes to interact persisted into the fourth week.) There was no teacher intervention in this grouping by sex on the first day. After that it was decided to start with some random groupings (for example, by assigning tags of one of three colors on one day and assembling on the basis of initial of first name on another). By the first Friday, the teachers had set up their own groupings on the basis of sex balance, balance of quiet and outgoing, balance of mature with those needing structure, and teacher preference for working with a child on the basis of established contact. This small group arrangement was used a good part of the time during the rest of the session, but there were a number of occasions when changes in groupings were made to serve specific ends.

The end of the second week saw the children fairly well acquainted with each other and mostly comfortable in the school setting. Now it was time to develop further group unity by planning for and going on a trip together. What happened in this regard provided some valuable learning experiences and warrants a certain amount of detailed recounting. On the second Thursday, children were assembled and told they could plan a trip, with the following limitations: three station wagons could be provided for transportation, everyone must go to the same place, no cost should be involved, and the entire trip must be completed within 2-1/2 hours. Consensus of the entire group must be reached by a certain hour or there would be no trip the next day. The children returned to their small groups to discuss alternatives and to be ready to report their suggestions to the large group. When the large group met again, the children were left on their own to go about reaching consensus. What ensued was chaos: children were shouting their own choices and decrying those of others; they made wholly irrelevant remarks; no one listened to anyone else; everyone talked at once, louder and louder, as it became apparent that no one else was listening. Occasional attempts at leadership were seen, as when someone would call for a vote, but results of a vote merely led to further divisiveness as children divided into camps in favor of one or another of the proposed activities. As the time deadline approached, it was apparent that no consensus would be reached. Many children were angry and indignant, and some of these kept turning to one or another of the teachers as if to say, "You let us down—we thought for sure we were going to have a trip and look what you let happen." It was apparent that none of them had thought about what behaviors on the part of members of a group are necessary if consensus is to be achieved; they had counted on adult intervention to help them out.

The next morning, children met in small groups and were asked to describe what had happened in yesterday's session: "No one listened," "Everyone talked at once," "There was no order," "It was like chickens running around." Next, children were asked to write down what things people would have to do to make such a session work out. A videotape had been made of the previous day's session, and the children assembled to watch it and note what kinds of helping or nonhelping behaviors they personally had shown. They were asked, "Was what you saw the way you want to be seen?" They were asked to state how they would change their behavior if they had it to do again. One boy, who had repeatedly made everyone laugh the day before by shouting, "Let's go to the sanitarium!" (when the planetarium was suggested), said, "I'll never make dumb remarks like that again when we're trying to decide something."

The children were then told they would have another chance at it. They returned to the small groups to talk over again what they might suggest as a trip destination and how they might each contribute to the achieving of consensus. When the large group met again, the teacher noted that anyone who really did not believe the group could come to an agreement was free to leave and find another activity. It was emphasized that this was perfectly all right for them to do, that teachers would consider it an entirely acceptable choice. They pointed out that if you really did not believe it could be done you probably would not be able to contribute anything to the group's attempt. All children chose to participate.

A list of five things to remember was put on the board:

Generate alternatives.
Consider more than one thing you could enjoy.
Try things that are helpful.
Be open to new ideas.
Self-interest is also group interest.

When the children were ready to bring up their suggestions and attempt to reach agreement, a teacher was available for some guidance, although he limited it to clarifying remarks: "Nikki is offering an alternative," "Caryn is supporting Nikki's suggestion," "John is asking for additional information," "Amanda is offering leadership in asking for a show of hands to see how close to agreement we are," and so on. The children's behavior was remarkably different from the previous day: they took turns in speaking; they paid attention to the ideas of others; they asked the group to listen to the suggestion of another ("I think Paul has something he wants to add," "Let Larry tell his idea").

Consensus was fairly easily achieved and the feelings of group unity had increased enormously. One boy who had been little involved with the group shouted, "It's the way the people felt when the astronauts landed safely!" To test whether children were just going along with the group decision because they didn't want a repeat of yesterday's unpleasantness, children wrote "yes" or "no" on unsigned ballots as to whether they had actually agreed with the decision. All wrote "yes."

Teachers used this consensus experience as a basis for further discussion of decision making and why sometimes consensus might be preferable to voting. Some children were able to extend the experience to the national and world level: "World problems might be solved if all the people talked it over and tried to decide on one thing everybody could agree to." Children were asked to tell how consensus and majority rule differ: "In majority rule, some of the people may have to do something they really don't want to." And, "It means there has to be some compromise usually—people might have to put in some *new* ideas."

This successful consensus experience was also videotaped, and the children watched it to see what each one of them had done toward making it work out ("Did I offer alternatives?" "Were my comments related?" "Did I offer leadership?" "Did I listen to others?") From then on, these bases of successful group participation were pointed out and reinforced when they did happen, and when someone did not show this behavior (did not listen, interrupted others, made irrelevant comments), this fact was pointed out as well. The development of effective group participation turned out to be one of the most successful results of the summer session.

Moving Beyond the Classroom

The third week saw the beginning of six encounters with children from a different cultural background. The group selected was a summer session drama class from the Wilmington Park Elementary School, whose enrollment was 70 percent Mexican-American and 20 percent black. The teachers and children were described as showing strong pride in self, family, and local community. They had been making their school a more humane place, with quality of interaction considered to be an important factor. For UES children, the exchange trips were meant to provide an opportunity to work with people of a different background; to identify likenesses and differences in values; and to welcome, value, and enjoy this diversity of background. For Wilmington Park the goals were somewhat similar. An additional focus for them was to provide their children with an opportunity to see that there are alternative job and living situations to which they could aspire.

In preparation for the trip, UES children were put into groups of four to work with problem plays in which they would have to consider a variety of solutions and then act out for the rest of the class the one they decided would be most appropriate. The idea was that when the two groups came together at Wilmington Park, the children would work together on such plays and thereby see how some of their values differed as they tried to work out solutions. However, the UES children had a good deal of difficulty with this activity just within their own group (being ill at ease and showing silly behavior), and so it was decided to try some simple mixed discussion groups instead.

On the first visit, the two groups met in a park near the Wilmington Park school. Activities provided included using the park equipment (swings, slide, sand) or playing softball or kickball. Children from both groups were reticent about making contact with each other. Varying degrees of involvement developed. At the highest level one might cite Colette, who immediately said, "Let's go get acquainted," and began to interact right away. She kept this up, calling the Mexican-American children by name, exploring the park with them, and taking one of the girls by the hand at refreshment time.

At another level, one could cite Lori, who, when it was gently pointed out that she was hanging back, said, "I've already met one." When asked about the kickball game she finally entered into with some of the Wilmington Park girls, she answered, "It was boring." Several of our children who had most freely expressed interest in peoples of the world and the larger problems of mankind were unable to interact. John D., quoted earlier for his high level of concern for his fellow man, did not join the Wilmington Park children in playing and eating. Instead, he hurried off to join a group of his UES friends in a private ball game. Amanda simply made a face when it was suggested they look for activities where they could interact with the others. She said, "I already know about Mexicans—we always have Mexican maids." When the Wilmington Park children served home-made tostados and guacamole refreshments, she turned up her nose, saying, "That doesn't look good."

Diaries of some of even the most thoughtful and mature of our children showed that making friends with the Chicano children was difficult:

> The first day I felt very uncomfortable. I asked one girl what she would like to play—kickball or softball—she gave no answer. I thought that was very cold but later I got to thinking maybe she was afraid to give her opinion because if we didn't like it she probably thought we'd put her down.

> I felt uncomfortable because I did a lot of the talking and I don't like Mexican food, but I didn't say anything that I felt. I like to get to know people but it was harder because they were a different race.

> I felt very strange because I didn't know anybody or the neighborhood.
>
> I thought children were supposed to be courteous and kind. They had an air of hostility toward everyone. They would only talk when spoken to. They didn't speak up and express themselves as you would expect from a drama class.

What we learned from this experience was that the ability to verbalize mankind sentiments is no guarantee of being able to act upon these sentiments. Children may be taught a great deal about other cultures, their values, their similarities and their differences, and so on, but as pointed out in Chapter 1, having intellectual grasp alone will not lead them to a truly mankind perspective.

The next day, our group returned to Wilmington Park to visit some of their school classrooms and then to have get-acquainted discussions. For the latter, the children were divided into four mixed groups, with a teacher serving as a nondirective leader. The going was slow, for the Wilmington Park children were very quiet and the UES children seemed baffled as to what was expected of them. Those who spoke out seemed to be saying what they thought the teacher wanted them to, rather than exploring their own thoughts and feelings and giving voice to them.

For our final visit, a more successful means of encouraging interaction and getting acquainted was carried out. Children were paired—one from UES and one from Wilmington Park—and interviewed each other for an About Me book. For the first time there were smiles, faces lighting up, expressions of interest and enthusiasm. At last we had found the level of operation at which to begin—a very concrete one where children could talk with each other about experiences they had in common. Talking about your brothers and sisters, your favorite song, your favorite food, and so on is much easier than going up to someone you do not know and trying to establish contact. Teachers noted that this is frequently hard even for adults and that perhaps we had been expecting too much initially from the children of both schools.

This last visit was productive for small group discussions when our group returned to UES. For instance, it was possible for children to note one difference, which was that most of the other children came from much larger families. One child commented, "Well, most Mexicans are Catholics, and that's the reason." Another added in a matter-of-fact tone, "Yes, they don't practice birth control." Someone else talked about other countries which were mainly Catholic: "My mother's family comes from Italy, and my aunts and uncles have very large families," and "My father's family used to be Catholic, and his parents both had lots of brothers and sisters." Thus the concrete experience of finding out about other children led to a discussion which took our children a step beyond their immediate selves, and discussion focused on bases of difference rather than on judgments regarding desirability of one difference over another.

The Wilmington Park children paid three visits to UES. For the first, the Name Game was played with great success. Given this structured task, the Wilmington Park children became less shy and entered into the naming with smiles and looks of triumph when they remembered names and when someone remembered their names. Then partners were assigned for the UES children to show their visitors around their school—the library, the woods, the gully—and to bring them juice and crackers. The visitors brought a piñata, and the day ended with a lively session as they all took turns swinging a big stick at the cardboard figure. Again on this occasion, some children sought to become better acquainted with their visitors, while others showed no inclination to do so. In fact, at one point, five of the UES children were seen playing a table game with their backs turned on a Mexican-American girl who was trying to join their group.

For their second visit, tours of UCLA were arranged, including a visit to the art building for a demonstration of throwing pottery and blowing glass. This did not encourage the interaction that was one of our goals, but it fulfilled the Wilmington Park goal of showing their children a university they might aspire to attend. Our teachers remarked, as they were walking with the children over the campus, about the kinds of things one could study here and what one had to do to gain entrance ("Finish high school, definitely, and do the best work you can").

On the final visit, all the children went swimming at the nearby women's gym and then returned for refreshments planned entirely by the UES children. Up until now, the UES children had been rather desultory in their involvement in planning for the Wilmington Park visits. This time, the teachers merely said, "What shall we do about refreshments tomorrow?" without any suggestions about what might be done. The growth of group responsibility and unity from the earlier weeks became apparent now. Committees were formed, responsibilities delegated, and lists made, without any direction whatsoever from teachers. The next day, there were ample hot pizzas, complete with numerous pizza cutters; there were pickles and popcorn and potato chips and cookies, paper plates and napkins and plastic forks. With no direction from teachers, the children set up the food on the patio and designed a way of serving to promote order and to assure that everyone was served before anyone had "seconds." Efficiently serving over fifty children without supervision took teamwork and planning, and the children carried it out with complete success.

An experience which undoubtedly helped the children recognize the need for this planning was one which teachers began setting up the very first day of school. The children had been told, casually, that the boxes in the cupboard contained the cracker supply for the entire six weeks. The next day, teachers had written on the board, "At the present rate of consumption our crackers will last three weeks. What can we do?" Teachers were interested to see if children would come up with some suggestions, showing recognition that in a group situation some kinds of rules are needed. No child had done so. With no rules or plans set up, the Wilmington Park children ate every remaining cracker on one of their visits. (Some took as many as twelve at a time.) The UES children were indignant, but someone pointed out, "Did we have a rule about that? Did we tell them there was any limit?" No more was said, but the incident was fresh in their minds when it came to planning for the next refreshments, and the UES children were going to be absolutely certain that such a thing did not happen again. We believe that had the teachers insisted the first few days that children work out some rules about cracker consumption, the lesson would not have been so well learned.

Special Problems

Before going on to the high point of the summer, the intensive living-together experience over the weekend in San Diego, it is appropriate to point out that all this did not come about entirely easily and smoothly. There were some rocky times along the way which required imaginative handling by the teachers. Early in the summer, it was evident that while a majority of the children were functioning well enough in the large and small groups, several boys continually behaved in a disruptive way. They poked each other, made unrelated comments, were inattentive and uncommitted. The observer was moved to note privately of one boy, "He's a pain in the neck; whines; is argumentative; interrupts; is selfish, self-centered, spoiled." Another child was noted to be sullen and disagreeable. Others could not commit themselves to anything, and they made the conduct of large and small group meetings difficult by their interruptions and distractibility. It was remarked in a team meeting that these boys could be whipped into shape easily enough if one chose to take the authoritarian route: silence them in the group, humiliate them by continually singling them out for criticism, threaten to send them home. After all, the remainder of the children were "good"—obedient, docile, and at least outwardly attentive—and one could argue that they deserved to get the full attention of the teachers.

But our teachers would not settle for writing off the seven disruptive boys. For a time groupings were changed, and two teachers worked intensively with the seven while the third teacher carried on with the rest. Teachers who met with the seven reflected with them that perhaps they were not ready for or were not interested in what the others in the group were doing, that perhaps they had not thought carefully enough about deciding to come to this summer school in the first place. Paul confirmed that this was true at least for him: "Right now I'd rather be at home playing with my friends and practicing baseball." Children were asked, "What can you plan for the rest of the summer that would make you want to stay? You know the goals: know what you value, know about yourself, then know something about others. How can we do this?"

Paul began to make irrelevant comments, and a teacher showed that she was a human being with feelings: "I'm taking what you say seriously, and I hope what you say is seriously presented." More silliness on Paul's part. The teacher added, "I'm here for real, not to goof off, and it makes me mad for you to." One or two of the boys began making suggestions, but again the others would not get involved. The teacher said, "You know what I'm trying to do? Get this group mobilized to do something it *wants* to do. I'm giving you a chance to consider some alternatives, so you can come to a decision— either as a group or as individuals—and I'm getting frustrated with you."

Finally, the group began to attend and warmly received Doug B.'s suggestion: "Have a group project. There should be at least two, maybe more, people together—not like working alone on About Me. I mean there should be some small groups that find some things they can do together, like making one big collage to decorate a whole wall." Others began to add to the idea: "We could have a theme, and each of the people could decide which part of the theme they wanted to work on." Another offered to bring some extra magazines from home to be sure they would have enough pictures from which to choose. Given the interest and attention of the teachers and their trust that the boys would be able to think of a worthwhile project to carry out, they soon got to work with enthusiasm.

Varying degrees of change were seen in the behavior of these boys. For George, perhaps a dim awareness that there are alternatives to settling conflicts besides tit-for-tat was a step forward. "He did it to me so I'll do it back" was a consistent pattern for George, as well as several others. One teacher spent a good deal of time having them think up several different ways that interaction might have ended besides "paying back," and then had them act these out. By the last week, George was still retaliating, but when asked what his behavior and that of his retaliating peers was like, he was able to say, "It's like nations."

One of the biggest changes of behavior was seen in Paul. He had been expelled from at least two schools for aggressive behavior and undoubtedly found school a punishing experience. But by the end of the summer session he stated that his mom was coming to visit the teachers and he, with her, was hoping that he could return in the fall as a regular UES student. His new involvement with his work and his participation in group activities were something truly exciting to see. His once sullen face was happy and relaxed, and he even found it possible to make friends with one of the teachers: "Hiya, Mr. Russell, how're things going for you today?" The rewards to teachers for spending this extra and sometimes difficult time with these boys were changes in behavior and attitudes such as these.

Meanwhile, total group planning and interaction continued. The evolving plan was to begin going deeper into a study of values and of people of differing cultures by means of literature and discussion. The teacher first read a story from Saroyan's *My Name Is Aram.* He stopped from time to time and asked, "What values are being shown? What can we tell about the people in the story?" Children were interested and made enthusiastic comments, but it was apparent that none could extract the deeper meanings of the story. On the next occasion, with a little more direct leading by the teacher, children were able to make somewhat more observant comments. But, by and large, in discussing their own values and what was important to them, children's perceptions and reactions remained on the concrete level. Even those with the highest professed commitment and with considerable verbal ability seemed unready to get sufficiently out of their own skins to empathize truly with a situation beyond their own immediate experience. It was agreed that probably *doing* and interacting were likely to be more productive at this stage than *talking about.*

Concluding Weeks

By the fifth week, the children were functioning so well, both as a group and as individuals, that one of the teachers invited the entire group to her home in San Diego for a long weekend. It had been hoped earlier that the summer program could include trips as long as two weeks at a time to permit much more intense interaction than is afforded in a short, daily session, but budgetary constraints had made this impossible. Consequently, the weekend trip to San

Diego was suggested instead. A letter home to parents gave the following list of goals which would receive major emphasis on the trip:

1. Students will help make a set of rules for the trip and, if necessary, will meet to discuss and change these rules as the weekend progresses.
2. Students will be encouraged to say what they think in a way so that others will listen. Thoughts might sound like:
   "I feel that...."
   "The way that I see it...."
   "It is my opinion that...."
3. Students will find out what other people think and feel.
4. Each student will work in a group that makes decisions by:
   saying what each thinks so that others will listen
   finding out what others think
   considering the consequences of what he and others wish to do
   considering other groups as an alternative for him.

It had been decided that if more than five of the group were unable to make the trip, we would not go. But nineteen signed up, and the trip was on.

Three station-wagon loads of children arrived in San Diego on Friday afternoon, and activity was continuous from then on until they left for home on Sunday afternoon. There was swimming, which went on continually from 3 in the afternoon until 9:30 at night the first day. A food committee accompanied a teacher to the store to pick out supplies for the evening meal and lunch the next day. Others were pressed into service for putting away groceries, getting the charcoal fire started, and setting the baked beans to simmering. No one was asked to do a certain job, but a call for volunteers was always enough to bring plenty of help. Children participated in cleanup after dinner, and then one carload went off to a baseball game while the rest stayed home and swam and cooked "Some-Mores" over the remains of the fire. Everyone had brought sleeping bags, and it was up to each child to find a sleeping place which suited him and which would not disturb anyone else. There were a few difficulties in deciding who would sleep where, but eventually all was quiet and everyone was asleep.

Next day, the children met to hear the different kinds of excursions they might choose for the day, and finally two cars went to the zoo and one to the Scripps Institute of Oceanography, to the beach at La Jolla, and to various waterfront attractions. Children had decided on the kinds of sandwiches they wanted to take along and had set up an assembly line sandwich production center. They again participated in supper preparations and cleanup and then chose to go on a Mystery Tour with one of the teachers or to stay home to swim, play games, and listen to stories. The next morning, though given a choice of further excursions, the children elected to stay there for a relaxed morning of swimming and games.

The children got along remarkably well, as had been anticipated. Deciding that one could put up and entertain this number of children comfortably, and even with pleasure, required much faith and trust in the children, and this was well justified. Teachers were more than enthusiastic about the outcome, saying that more had been accomplished over the weekend than had been done in the first five weeks. Children were put in a position of having to face any conflicts which came up rather than running away from them as they could do in a three-hour daily session. Children had to think continually about how their behavior was affecting others, whether they were helping or hindering the pleasure of the rest of the group.

Only one child found she was not up to this. She had been cheerful, lively, and outgoing during the summer school session, and teachers had no reason to anticipate that she would have difficulties. But her constant need to be noticed, her baiting and teasing and manipulativeness, and her inability to recognize or own up to her responsibility for the unpleasant consequences could not go unnoticed when the time period was prolonged and the interaction sustained. One thing learned here was that the outward patina of proper socialization should not mislead teachers about actual level of ego development. This child might have benefited more from her summer school experiences had teachers had an opportunity to become aware earlier of her self-defeating behavior. To have done so, though, would have required the time and intensity of the San Diego experience.

A happier picture, and an impressive one, was of a laughing Lynne (the shyest and most retiring child during the first weeks) riding fully clothed across the swimming pool on the shoulders of one of the boys. The boy commented, "Well, when someone trusts you like that you have to be sure and take good care of them."

The final weeks following the San Diego weekend showed a group of children working both alone and together with the greatest of enthusiasm and productiveness. Teachers had decided to set up special interest groups for the last week of school, so that in choosing to participate in one or another of them, children would be making a decision of some consequence to them. Activities offered were drama, literature, and art, and once a child decided, he would work with a group on that activity for the first hour and a half of the morning and, if he wanted, could continue on with it during Choice. After children had chosen, a very high degree of involvement was observed.

Marc, who throughout had been almost entirely uninvolved in anything that was happening, so totally inattentive that one might have thought he was somewhat backward intellectually except for the occasional intelligent comment he made, now set to work in drama with a vengeance. The children worked on two plays a morning, one a problem play for which they had to think and act out some alternative endings, and one a play that was just for fun. The problem plays were acted out each day for the rest of the group. Marc became talkative, enthusiastic, and highly assertive. That he had been attending to what had been going on was attested to by a comment he made to one of his fellow drama students when they were busy making props for one of their plays: "John, I gave you your choice. Now which one are you going to do?" The drama group worked so well that by the end of the week they were able to perform for others without giggling and laughing, speaking up in strong voices and getting their point across effectively.

The children who chose literature (with a focus on people of different backgrounds) were interested and involved. In earlier group discussions of stories, children had seemed satisfied to wait for the teacher's explanations or to hear one suggestion from another child and then agree with it. Now they were willing to think up several alternatives as to why someone behaved in a certain way and to discuss these freely. Jill was talking more than she had throughout the session, and Herbie said he had now found something he really liked to do. John D. mentioned this activity as a main highlight of the summer for him.

The majority of children had chosen art. Each day a new technique was introduced, and the great care children took with their work was evidence of their pride in what they were doing. Here was something that was worth their care. Paul, who had not spent much time at any one thing, spent the full hour and a half every day doing his art work, completing one project and enthusiastically starting a second. His own feelings of pride and pleasure now permitted him to go around saying, "Hey, Matt, that really looks good....Dave, I really like yours." Formerly stolid little Lori could not conceal the delight she felt when the teacher held her work up at a distance so that she could see how it looked. Her expression said, "Is it really all right for me to be proud of myself?" Rob, who had shown interest in nothing but sports, worked one day all through the first hour and a half, through Choice, and on through the last hour, saying, "I want to get this finished so I can take it home."

Teachers had said a week or two earlier, "These children are tired of talk—we need to have them at work together on projects." The success of the last week's special interest activities suggested that they probably were right.

One other thing was happening during this last week. There were secret conversations, furtive looks, lists being passed about. The final day of school disclosed what it was all about: a thank-you party for their teachers. Teachers were drawn out of the room by one ruse or another: two girls needed to talk over something with Mrs. Lee privately; the drama group wanted Mr. Lewis for some last-minute rehearsal; Lynne asked Mr. Russell to go to the library with her to talk over some books. With them out of the way, a watermelon materialized from behind the blocks in the cupboard; a cake made by one of the girls appeared out of a closet; handmade favors for the teachers were produced; curtains were drawn; the tables and desks were pulled together to make one large banquet table; and streamers were festooned all across the room. The children assembled in the banquet room, and not a sound was heard from any of them—not even from the boys who earlier could have been counted on to giggle and shout and spoil the surprise. Again, they had acted smoothly and effectively as a group and had worked together to do something to give pleasure to other people. Perhaps they had taken only one small step toward a truly mankind perspective, but no one could doubt that they were on their way!

The Children Comment

Because just recounting the events of the summer cannot give the full flavor and the extent of the impact on the children, we are adding here some statements from the children themselves. On concluding days, the observer asked each child to speak into a tape recorder about how summer school had been for him, what he thought about it, and what his impressions were. Here are some of the things they said:

> The kids are nice, and you aren't forced to make any answer, and the teachers are really good. And I think to go to this school in the regular school would be great.... It's just a really great school here. Every day you do something different. Like at my other school we used to do the same things day after day. And this school is just a lot better. And the work is sometimes challenging to your brain—that's good for you I guess.... I like the way the teachers *explain* everything, instead of just saying "you do this and that," and just leave you. And Mr. Russell and Mrs. Lee, and well, just all the teachers have been very nice to me. They've been open...if you do something wrong. They do interesting things...like today in Mr. Russell's group when we were doing reading, about every few minutes Mr. Russell would stop and ask, "Why do you think he did this?" or "How do you think he feels?" *(John D.)*

> Well, I have enjoyed UES very much, and I enjoy the freedom, doing whatever you want, just don't exceed the limits. And I enjoyed the teachers very much, and I thought they were very considerate. I enjoyed the program very much because we got to do things we wanted in the subjects we chose. And I've learned a lot about the other people in this class and what they like and what they want to do. And I've also learned that we can learn together without

very many rules. I would like very much to come back to this class again. I think this was a very nice program for those who like to express themselves. *(Jill)*

I like the freedom, and the other stuff like choice time when we had our own choice to do things and we could go different places, like the forest area. And the teachers at UES, the trust that they gave us, and the trust the students gave us. . . . And the people here know everybody else, because it's a closely related school. And I like this school because there's a lot of freedom in it, and you can do whatever you want at a certain time when there's a teacher around, and that's different from my school. All we can do is just go to this stupid yard. Here you can play basketball, you can go into the forest area, you can wrestle, and there's a gully you can explore, and you can ride your bikes here, and you don't have any detention hall when you get into trouble. . . . And the people here are much nicer. You can do a lot more stuff that you please, and it's a lot funner to do what you want, because if you do what you want, you learn more. *(Dave)*

Well, I like this school, and the activities and everything that they have, like the Blind Walk we had, and levitation. . . . And I've got to know lots of people, how they react to different things, much better. And I like the forest and gully here. It reminds me of forests, of real forests, rather. . . . And I like to be free, and here I think they are trying to teach you all sorts of things, like freedom and how it is to be free. *(Colette)*

The thing I like most about summer school is that it's fun. And other things are new, like how are you going to make friends better— it's easier to make friends. And there's acting to do, I just *love*. It's pretty hard, and me and Cornell try our best. . . . Anyhow, who do you know who has a good friend? Like I got Cornell, he's my faithful friend, you know? Let me tell you, I really like summer school. Yeah! Because it's so fun. I don't get in fights as much as I do in regular school, things like that really help, you know? I like summer school because, well, I'd like to know *your* impressions about it. Do you or do you not *like* it? Well, I like it. . . . If *you* don't like it, that's okay, 'cause everything is okay. Like, my teacher—he's real fun, you know? Have you ever tried making a play on your *own*? Well, I have, five times. I always practice at home. I usually just goof around at home, but now I practice at home because it's *fun* to do it. And when it's fun to do it, you know it's fun....I hope you like it too....You know, this is the most *fun* summer I have ever had? So, I hope that *you* like it. If you don't, oh, brother. That would be the worst thing in the world to know. It's a nice time, it's a *nice* time. Well, this is it—I'll be seeing ya, all right? You see, it's really fun—at *this* school it is. *(Marc, the silent one)*

Well, the first thing I thought was important was that we went to a park and met different people, that were different in different ways...like some were Mexican and some were black...and I really learned something about that. It was fun to make friends with them. I met a boy named Andrew....I felt I made friends with him, and I felt good inside....Also, the situation plays help you learn to find out ways you can solve things...and I enjoyed that. *(John U.)*

I think that when we went and visited the Wilmington Park people I don't think we should have visited them because they weren't all that fun, to really visit. I think we should have visited somebody else that would have been talkative like us, you know, more like us. Maybe a different race, but more like us. *(Nikki)*

I liked getting experienced with the other people, and to know what they're like. And going to the Wilmington Park school and having a chance to see how other people do in school, what they are like, and how their classrooms are. And we got to know other people and see how they work, how they work in the class, in the group. And I like to express my own opinion in as many ways as I can, so it gave me a big chance to. And I will try to go next summer. *(Caryn)*

Well, I thought the summer was good. I liked doing art. I like learning about myself, and what I like to do. And I think the teachers are really nice. *(Lynne)*

We've been to some real neat places. At my other school we haven't been to these places. There are really neat people in this class. And it was real fun in San Diego, and it was nice of Mrs. Lee to invite us over at her house....And last year at my summer school they didn't have recess or anything. This is a much better school....And I learned a lot about the world, and what's happening, and about the kids in our class, about each other....It was fun meeting the kids from Wilmington, and it was fun going swimming with them, and it was interesting meeting them, getting to know each other. I met five people there. And it was interesting because

they started to catch on, started talking, after they were with us a couple of days—because, you know, they were pretty shy. *(Rob)*
I like the time when we went on our trip to San Diego. But before we did that, at our summer school we got acquainted, and I liked that, to get acquainted and know each other. We had the Name Game, and after we all got acquainted, we had groups, we had Choice, and then we'd go to our groups and do our special stuff. And, well, there was nothing I didn't like. *(Lori)*
I *love* this school, and I wish I could go the entire year. I've learned about a whole bunch of things....I'm more honest than I used to be....I think this is one of the nicest years I've ever had....You learn about yourself, more than you did know before, the things you never even thought about before. You have six weeks of this great stuff, and get to really enjoy it. *(Esme)*
The best part was when we went to San Diego! Man, that was *neat!* And I just got through with an *art project.* And if you don't think that was good you should have seen it. We just got back from San Diego—it was cool. The best part of the summer is...right now, the last week where we're working on art. Yesterday we worked on an art project in clay—we made anything, some kind of imaginary object that's an animal. I think this is real good, and I might be coming to this school sometime soon. *(Paul)*
So far I haven't learned too much. The interesting thing we did was going to Wilmington. I liked going to this summer program—I don't think I could have thought of anything better to do. I have some impressions—Cornell is a nut and George is an absolute maniac. I've gotten real sock of a few people....Right now 'bout the only time I can really enjoy myself is when I'm alone in the woods, with my stick....I'm in the literature group, and I like doing that, listening to stories....I've found a couple of good books....That's about all. *(Herbie)*
This school is pretty good, because you know, we do things that I never did at my other school. We did painting, and different kinds of things. We did a fun project—that was an About Me book....I had a real good time—it was *different.* It was great—everything we had going for us; we had a forest, we had the playground, we had the indoor rooms, we had everything you could think of. I mean, this is really a great school, and I liked the teachers, and I liked the trip to San Diego—that was the best thing all year. *(Mike)*

I *like* UES, it's a fine place to *be*! I enjoy walking in the woods, and stuff like that....I like your library pretty good, and I like some of the books you had. And the playlets we got to do; I like doing the playlets. I enjoyed, I enjoyed, I enjoyed! *(Cornell)*

I thought the program was fun and everything, and I learned about myself, and about other people, and I made friends. And the teachers are really nice. You have more freedom than you usually do, and you don't have to be disciplined. I really liked the field trips and everything. It was just fun, I guess. It would be pretty good if they could continue the class next year—I'll come back. So if you want to know about doing the class again, do it again. *(Amanda)*

I like this summer. I came to UES and I thought this class was going to be dull, but it turned out to be fun. And I'm doing a lot of good things here....We don't have to do any really hard work, mostly we did art and went on trips. I learned a lot in this class....and I could make friends easier than I do at my other school. And I wish we could stay here a whole year. *(George)*

I didn't think it would be like this, like it was. In my regular school you just do work....I just didn't think it would be *like* this....I didn't think we'd have any art...and I'm in the art class. Well, it's fun. What I thought of UES? Well, I didn't think I was going to....Well, it's more than I expected. *(Kelly)*

I've had fun and I've made friends and I liked the teachers. I like the work they do, 'cause they're not strict or anything. I wish this summer school would go on longer. I like the things we do—we've gone on trips and we could do art, and reading, and the About Me project is fun. There's special activities you don't have at normal school—like the trips and going to San Diego and visiting other schools, and learning how to meet people. *(Larry)*

I like the summer school a lot, and I don't think anything could be changed; I don't think we need to spoil it, because it's really good....I like the teachers and I like the kids. I went one time before, but this is the best time I've ever had here. I go to regular school here—it's just about as good as you can get. I wouldn't go to any other school, if I had a choice. The summer school was good, and I hope I can go next year. *(Laura)*

I think it was worthwhile and I liked it very much because I like the teachers and the kids, and we all got to trust each other by the things that we did. We all got to know about each other by the games we played. And I think I've learned a lot of different things that I didn't know before about me—and about other people. The About Me project was meaningful to me because we did a lot of fun things with it. And I liked the way we got into small groups and had discussions and stuff. I wish that I could have brought up more alternatives and suggestions in the discussion group. Maybe people thought I didn't care, but I did—I just didn't say much. . . . I really thought this summer was special, and I'll probably always remember it. I really like the teachers, I really like the system of teaching, and I wish I could have gone here for the regular school year. *(Adrianne)*

Well, this school is good 'cause the teachers are nice and they really don't press you to do anything except sometimes they do. When you're wondering, when you have a problem choosing, they help you, and they're really good teachers, the best teachers I've ever had. . . . And we always do a lot of things, and we have a half hour of Choice, which is really fun. 'Cause at a regular school, usually at a school you have to do one specific game, but not at UES. It's just different from regular schools. You can read whenever you want, you can do art during Choice, you can read during Choice and you can play, and you can wrestle, you can do a lot of things. . . . In discussion groups when we're deciding where we're going to go on trips it's fun, because you've got to reach a consensus and it's really fun to talk. And when the teachers call us to meet our small groups, we discuss what we're going to do and about things that you did, and what you did during Choice, and what you want to do this next half hour. Someone says, "I'm going to read," and I said, "I'm going to do art," so it's really good because you can pick what you want to do. And the teachers, when you talk to them, they listen. And they say to the kids, "Did you hear what that person said?" And if they say "No," you just repeat it, and then maybe they'll say it's a good idea. And the teachers, they'll listen to you and they talk back—they talk back to you not in a mean way but they talk back in a nice way. They'll say, "Oh, that's good," things like that, so you don't feel embarrassed. . . . This is the best school I've been to, and I wish I could keep the teachers. *(Matt)*

The Teachers Reflect

This chapter concludes with some retrospective thoughts of the teaching staff. What follows are the direct quotes of teachers, with quotation marks removed, woven together into a composite commentary.

As the summer of '71 was drawing close, I became increasingly concerned that we would not have enough planned in specific terms to provide activities that were sufficiently vivid and different, that were meaningful to the children, and that truly led to a mankind perspective. I was reasonably comfortable proceeding to the day-to-day planning only because I would be working with two highly competent colleagues whom I greatly respected and with whom communication was easily effected. I would not be willing at this point to try to implement, or replicate, the project on my own in a self-contained classroom, in either summer or regular session. There is still too much that needs to be worked out in a team setting, and a team approach is the desired method of proceeding.

The complexity of the project and the fuzziness of the concepts required optimum conditions for curriculum design. One of the significant aspects of the project was the interaction during the planning stage of people from a wide range of backgrounds. The limitations of each person in terms of perspective and ideas were greatly offset by the numerous, lengthy discussions.

A second asset of the planning phase was the large amount of time available for planning over a long period of time. Being able to set aside large blocks of time, a full day or a day and a half or several successive days, allowed ideas and topics to be fully discussed. Often the full impact of an idea did not occur for several hours—long after the usual after-school meeting would have been concluded.

It is important to point out that in order to maximize the possibility of providing a powerful learning environment dealing with largely untried curricula, a low child-teacher ratio is an important factor. We question whether such a program could be duplicated with equal effectiveness, given a greater number of pupils for each teacher. Perhaps students progressing through a school which explicitly emphasizes the behaviors sought would, after a number of years, come to have less need of the close support and guidance included in our plans. We are not willing to so conclude at this time.

Transcendence of self is something worth attempting with children of this age. Several in the group were beginning to see beyond themselves, and each child was working along the continuum of self-transcendence. This particular objective has great meaning for both teachers and children. The continuum starts with knowledge of self.

My recommendations for another teaching session would be:

First Phase: Extensive work with things that illustrate knowledge of self to each person in the group. About Me could again be an excellent activity. Many lists of strengths, weaknesses, likes, dislikes, physical characteristics, family traits, projective stories, learnings achieved thus far in life, goals for the future, view of self in different situations—in large groups, by self, with peers—should be arranged and written down. Each person should have an opportunity to compare his data—that which is not private—with several other people of his own age and those younger and older. This would begin to give a child some idea of where he has been, where he is now, and where he is going.

Concurrent with the self, it is desirable to have many experiences in learning about other members of the group: names, likes, dislikes, etc. Children should be helped to explore what makes friends, what makes enemies, what a person does to meet someone new. This portion could be developed with name games, listening activities, work projects, and then detailed discussion and summary of the results of the interaction with another person. Short trips in informal settings should be taken where the skills identified in the group setting might be tried out—making friends, doing something with someone you don't know, asking questions of new persons, and so on.

As a result of this first phase, a child probably would have a strong idea about himself—surely always to be added to but with some good base data and also knowledge of himself in relation to one or two others in the group. He would also gain knowledge about the other members in the group.

Second Phase: Several longer trips would be planned for the group as a whole. During these times, the things learned about self and one or two others would be given a chance to develop. What do you have in common with others on a longer trip? What happens when you have a disagreement with a friend? What does each individual and the group do about those who don't do their share of the work? The goal of these longer trips would be to try out what each child found out about himself in the first phase and to continue to add to the data about his interactions in different work and play situations.

Third Phase: The group would meet to study about a group of children quite similar to themselves. A trip to another school of like background would be taken, with interviews, group games, play and work situations, and short trips.

A succeeding part of this phase would be one or more lengthy interaction-study situations with groups of children of widely differing backgrounds from the children in the original class. All of the skills that had been identified and strengthened would come into play. Making friends, learning about someone who is different, participating in the activities of a different culture, and inviting another person to participate in one's own culture would be the focus of this phase.

Things to Change: In any random grouping, some children would work on the activities that give knowledge about self for the whole period while other children would go through phases one, two, and three. Not all children would go through all phases together. This is as obvious in mankind studies as it is in the study of mathematics; some children have farther to go than others and will take different routes.

I feel I interacted with children in new ways. I was closer to them than I had been with children in the past. I had time to be with them as a human being and not just as a teacher with something to "teach" or to put out for them to take in. There seemed to be so much happening as a result of the process. I was listening to children as I had never listened before. I was fascinated and enchanted by their views of the world, their friends, and people they knew. I was fascinated by the scope of their awareness and concerns. I was intrigued to find out what was important to them. I spent more and more of my time absorbing what children were saying, feeling, and doing, and less time "putting out."

Expressing my fascination and genuine interest conveyed a sense of worthiness to the children. They knew I cared about them and their values. They knew I liked them and would spend time with them. They became more open and expressive as they realized that what they felt and thought was important to me. I think they began to value their own views and ideas as valid or worth someone else's consideration.

I spent a good deal of time looking at school, learning, and teachers through the eyes of the children. Listening more closely also gave me insight into the children's value systems. Our values and theirs are often quite different. But how often do we stop to find out what they value? What they value directly affects what they say and do. When we fail to discover how they view a situation or what values they are going by, we usually assume that they are operating under *our* value system. Therefore, we just consider their behavior inappropriate or deviant.

I see educators demanding all sorts of accountability and trust of children with little thought as to how we are accountable to them or trusting of them. Often we use our power as adults in control to make excuses for not carrying through plans and promises. To the child this appears to be an expression of our inability to keep our word.

We expect a huge amount of trust from children. They trust us with all kinds of decisions that affect their lives and feelings. But how much do we trust them? What results from trusting them? How do they begin to feel when they are trusted? How does their behavior change? One boy this summer said it several times: "When you know someone trusts you, you try not to let him down."

My interaction with children is a major area of change for me. It became more personal and intimate and included a much larger range of areas. I *look* at children differently now. I see them as being more capable of making important decisions. Somehow it is easier for me to accept their values, especially when expression of their values contradicts or threatens my ideas or plans. It is much easier to accept their complaints or objections. And usually they are legitimate, valid, usable, and sensible observations.

I have learned to maintain respect for a child even though his behavior angers me. There seemed to be no conflict with the feelings of "I'm really angry with you!" and "You are a beautiful child!" I felt strongly that the children perceived this message in that they could accept my feelings without feeling that I was rejecting them as persons. This attitude is due to three factors. First, I was able to more clearly see their value system. Second, I could maintain the attitude that there was a legitimate reason for their behavior. They were acting out real and legitimate feelings, not being naughty! And finally, I was able to view their expressions of feelings and behaviors as part of a learning process rather than an obstacle to what had to be learned. The low child-teacher ratio gave time and energy to deal with their values and perceptions here and now, and I didn't have to feel that dealing with these things was interrupting something more important.

Children responded to the above by saying things like: "You can express what you really think; you can choose the things you like to do; you feel important when you can decide on what you're going to do and who you can work with; the teachers here are interested in you and they really care about how you feel."

They also responded toward each other in more caring and respecting ways. They accepted others' differences without being judgmental. For instance, many said things like: "The kids from Wilmington Park were quiet and shy and it was hard to get to know them." This is a nonjudgmental statement of fact. To me this is evidence of a very positive direction in which these children had begun to move.

There was also a big difference in the way we three teachers worked together. We were much more accepting of the values and feelings of ourselves and our teammates. The three of us had worked together many times before, but now we more openly expressed doubts, fears, and negative feelings as well as positive ones. We could see our failures, talk about them, and express how we felt. We were also able to forgive ourselves and even express to the children how we felt about our mistakes. We could accept our shortcomings and not lose sight of our strengths. We received a great deal of comfort and support from each other. This gave us courage to risk new ideas and try new approaches with the children. We could admit our ambiguous feelings and our indecision, knowing the other two either felt the same way or could easily see our point of view.

I view this summer program, including the year and a half of planning time, as the most significant learning and growing experience of my teaching career. I grew as a person relating to children and also as a person relating to fellow teachers. I've seen clear and positive results from genuine and honest interrelationships with children and teachers. This process is growth-producing in many ways. As one little girl put it: "You learn more about yourself, more than you did know before, some things you never even thought about before."

Notes

1. *Webster's Third New International Dictionary,* definition 3.

Chapter 7
Reflections

We entered into what has been described on preceding pages as an inquiry, hoping to learn a little about the meaning of the mankind idea and especially about its potential as a unifying concept in the education of children. Our experience has taught us that the road toward a mankind school is difficult to travel albeit rewarding. Not only did we have difficulty grasping the idea in all its power and, ironically, simplicity, but, in addition, we had difficulty translating it into a framework for schooling. Then, personal, human frailties ccmpounded the problems of actually implementing this framework in practice.

We begin this concluding chapter by reflecting on our experience in the hope of helping others interested in pursuing similar goals. The time period involved in the endeavors previously described coincided almost precisely with the time period of a study designed to gain insight into processes of changing schools in which most of us participated.[1] Consequently, we are able to draw on the latter, too, in developing suggestions for educators who would seek to change their schools toward a mankind orientation.

On Schooling for Mankind

We assume that mankind concepts and processes are learned and that the schools can and should play a significant part in this learning. But simply to slip them into the program of existing schools, as a sort of curricular cassette, will achieve little. Clearly, for the mankind concepts discussed here to catch hold in the schools, to say nothing of flourish, will require radical reconstruction of the human relationships in them, of the concept and function of the institution, of the content, and of the attitudes and behavior of teachers. We are talking about basic reorientation of both individuals and institutions. Nothing is more difficult.

But is it reasonable to assume that the schools can become crucibles for education oriented toward mankind goals? To the dismay of most of us who have had considerable faith in our schools, evidence is mounting to the effect that "schools might best be regarded as passive reinforcers of abilities, aspirations and values established elsewhere."[2] Can the school, then, become a countervailing force of sufficient influence to offset the threats to mankind? Can it become a significant force for mankind?

To expect the school to stand alone against the destructive tendencies of society is to expect what never has been and, probably, never will be. We can only hope that the school will become one of several constructive forces striving for a better world for all mankind. Such forces exist, just as they always have existed, weakly or vigorously. For those who are educators, school presents an opportunity to join with these forces.

Grasping the opportunity means making the assumption that schools can make a difference, even in attempting something as complex as promoting the idea of mankind. There are contradictory charges and claims regarding the potency of the school. One group of critics argues, citing supporting evidence, that traditional inputs of funds, class size, curriculum, and the like do not seem to change, fundamentally, the course of pupil behavior.[3] The school appears not to be responsive—"a school is a school is a school." Other aspects of pupil life are more influential, apparently, and are brought into the school where they continue to be more powerful than "school" efforts.

By contrast, however, a formidable array of critics condemns the schools *for* its influence, maintaining that it suppresses individuality, selects and sorts for predetermined roles in society, and is an inhumane place unfit for guiding the malleable child. For these critics, changing the curriculum or patterns of educating teachers will not suffice—the school must be abolished completely. It is to be replaced by parents, tutors, work experiences, and a host of informal, direct-encounter educational activities.

Critics of differing beliefs come together, then, in condemning the school, one group for its impotence and the other for its powerful, misdirected shaping. Out of such divergent criticism is emerging a rhetoric of deschooling running counter to our past rhetoric of faith in the schools.[4] Research is being reinterpreted and case studies cited to give substance to this rhetoric. In the wake of the rhetoric have come counterschools—a variety of schools "free" of the restraints of organized public education and "free" in the sense of departing from many of the prescribed routines, including curricula, normally accompanying regular schools.[5]

Once the rhetoric addresses itself to proposals rather than criticism, however, there is considerable, often heated, disagreement over directions for change. The counterschools reflect this disagreement. Perhaps this is one of the reasons why most of them are so short-lived; even the few people involved in the smallest schools agree on little beyond a few generalizations. Those that survive longer often begin to suffer from rigid institutionalization of the agreements needed to keep an institution alive. Note this description from one who wanted to view these schools through sympathetic eyes:

> Whether for the sake of principle or necessity, counterschools often promote a relentless sociability. Where this produces openness, tolerance and cooperative enterprise, it can scarcely be faulted. But just as often it operates to deny privacy, silence and sustained purpose. Or if not denied, these luxuries must be protected by a system of rules no less onerous for being self-imposed. In institutions enrolling a wide age range, the youngest children are likely to be repeatedly summoned before the school judiciary for petty infractions of quiet hours and silent zones. Teachers, of course, are subject as much as students to interruption, harassment and distraction. Consequently,

those adult models of persistent and disciplined purpose which might invite emulation are seldom evident.[6]

It appears that if schools did not exist, people would invent them anyway. Merely creating new schools is no guarantee that they will be more humane, more oriented toward man and mankind. We should proceed with the reconstruction of those we have.

Whether schools are public or private, "free" or part of a larger system, there needs to be agreement on assumptions, goals, a conceptual framework to guide discussions, and the kinds of activities that are to go on there. As we have seen, such agreements are hard to come by; they require, among other things, ideas and disciplined group interaction. Perhaps this is why so few schools have guiding agreements.[7] Simply to say that we want a "humanistic school" or a "child-centered school" is to indulge in slogans. Goals, processes, and substance must be defined through sustained effort. We propose that these may be found in the idea of mankind.

But those who question the potency of the schools return us full cycle to our question, can the schools be a significant force for mankind? The evidence sometimes mounted to question the power and effectiveness of the school is sufficiently formidable to cause us to despair, especially over attempting anything so complex as promoting the idea of mankind in such a place. But let us look more closely. Several limitations may be noted in studies and projects which have been cited as demonstrating that what happens in school does not make much difference.

Frequently, these studies deal with only a small part of a problem and so simply lack the power to make much difference. To assume that project A or B will make much difference too often is akin to assuming that attaching a 35-horsepower outboard motor to the hull of a 50,000-ton vessel will propel such a ship at significantly faster speeds. Other projects designed to change schools focus oh intervening variables only indirectly related to the output variables ultimately measured. For example, team teaching may have some direct effect on teacher comfort or discomfort or on patterns of educating teachers—outputs probably not measured—but little or no impact on pupil achievement, the output factor tested. Consequently, the interaction may be deemed ineffective for failing to do what it was not intended to do. Or, with other projects, perhaps insufficient time was allowed for the intended changes to manifest themselves. Just as significant changes were about to appear, the evaluators completed their work, packed up their questionnaires, and began to write their report.

Schools are complex social systems made up of many interacting parts. Interventions focused on a few of these parts cannot be expected to make much difference. Changing the general method of teaching reading, for example, has a limited impact on general achievement scores in reading, although such a change may move individual children up or down on the reading scale. It seems reasonable to assume that complex institutions require complex, powerful strategies for their reconstruction.

We believe that schools do make a difference—less than some people claim, more than others believe—and could do much more. That other influences are also powerful—especially home, community, and television—must not be denied. Schools are reasonably effective in teaching an array of basic skills and subject matter. With allowances for the complexity of subject matter in relation to pupil maturity, children learn what they are taught, even when the material to which they are exposed normally is reserved for higher grades in the system. Furthermore, the school encourages or suppresses talent, extinguishes some behaviors in favor of others, develops impressions of what is right and wrong, and imprints lifelong memories of "school." We are not prepared to write it off, for either its impotence or its malevolence, while recognizing that it is characterized by some of both. We want to employ its resources in the interests of mankind.

On Changing Schools for Mankind Purposes

Our studies have indicated that in order for the school to be successful in bringing about the changes it intends, things have to happen on two levels. There first must be processes within the school (among the principal, staff, students, and parents) which create an atmosphere conducive to the establishment of mankind ideas and which press for change. In addition there must be some system of outside support which encourages the school to continue in its search for new paths. We deal first with the internal processes of the school.

Working within the School

Of primary importance is the existence of a "critical mass" of responsible persons—preferably children, parents, teachers, principal—committed to exploring mankind concepts and their implications for schooling. It is not necessary, we think, to have an entire school faculty committed at the outset. There is danger that such full-scale "commitment" would be superficial, given the fact that school faculties usually are unable to agree on basic values or goals for a school. But a small dedicated nucleus prepared to devote much time and energy and to agree to disagree is imperative. If the work prospers, their enthusiasm will be contagious; others will join of their own free will in due time.

Second, our experience with the experimental program described in Chapters 5 and 6 indicates that the common tendency to seek early closure on "doing something" should be resisted. The ideas and concepts must become natural not only in general discourse but also in discussions geared more specifically to practical applications. A useful exercise is that of separating what is parochial from what is mankind. Dealing with problems of truancy from school is a parochial problem; concern for educational opportunity geared to the needs of all is a mankind problem. Disposal of household garbage is a parochial problem; what to do about pollution of the stratosphere and the oceans is a mankind concern. The parochial problems are personal and are readily grasped and understood; they provide convenient bridges to a mankind perspective.

The intent at these initial stages is to provide frequent total immersion in the mankind idea and its possible implications. This requires extensive reading and ample opportunities to discuss what is read. We recommend that some of this reading be in common, with varying interpretations subjected to sharp analysis. For this purpose, attention is directed especially to the publications of the Council for the Study of Mankind, Inc. (authors and editors such as Hirschfeld, Ulich, and

Wagar). Also, we have included in this volume an annotated bibliography of useful resources. It is essential that a small library of basic references be established.

Next, the study group should agree on and hold to a set of operational ground rules: meetings must be regular; there must be an agenda; attendance must be regular; all must be read. There should be a deliberate process of self-analysis. Are we reading adequately? Do reports on this reading go to the heart of things? Do we listen to each other? Do we challenge viewpoints without attacking persons? Do we set between-meeting tasks? Do we have a process for reporting progress, problems, shortcomings, etc., following each meeting? All of these points apply to any group processes, of course, not just to inquiry into the mankind idea. School groups will vary enormously in their ability to proceed in ordered ways, but all can and will improve if they take the process seriously. Some simply will fall by the wayside; disciplined group work is not for them.

Then, in time, at least a feeling for the idea of mankind will emerge. There is no need to attempt definitions; in fact, such exercises are likely to end in frustration and failure. The very best minds have tried and failed. To sense or intuit what it means to have a mankind perspective is sufficient. To think and act from this intuitive orientation is the goal.

The process described so far may go on for a year or more without there being any move toward a program or a plan for a mankind school. It lasted much longer than this for us, but, admittedly, we had formed two related communicating discussion groups by the end of the first year—one preoccupied primarily with developing a framework for a total school, the other with agreeing on a trial project. The two came together for a kind of mutual "correction" to be sure that the framework was useful and that the project reflected it.

Our experience raises an important procedural question. Is it better to stay with the total immersion discussion process until considerable understanding is realized, eschewing practical implications? Or is it better to get started relatively soon with some practical proposal, using this as a vehicle for exploring what it means to think and act in mankind terms? We are inclined to stay with our earlier warning:

that is, it is unwise to get early closure on a project. However, this does not preclude the usefulness of focusing early on specific educational applications of the mankind idea in order to translate general concepts into more tangible meaning. Examples are examined against a background of the class of things to which they belong, both taking on clearer meaning in the process. The purpose of this is to enhance a dialogue leading, in turn, to greater understanding. It stops short of action.

Ultimately, out of this process should come several suggestions for actual practice. We proposed, explored, and rejected several before settling on the one described in Chapters 5 and 6. The one finally agreed to did not meet with uniform enthusiasm and, in fact, was a compromise for all of us, a compromise in which a number of practical considerations won out over such factors as potential power and challenge of proposed interventions. Because of the conceptual difficulty we had experienced, staying on at least partially familiar ground in order to enhance success seemed important. We are inclined to caution others likewise, especially since few groups are likely to spend as much time as we did on the contextual background or to have had more classroom experience. All of the teachers in our team were accustomed to working in demonstration situations and teacher education programs.

Even though we caution against tackling too much at the outset, urging that a good deal of what is familiar be retained in venturing into the unfamiliar, a caveat of some importance is in order here. We are talking about creating mankind schools, not simply tacking on a new unit of instruction to be incorporated into an otherwise unchanged program. Admittedly, we dealt directly with only one component of our four-part framework—namely, human interaction involving humanistic interpersonal relations and certain self-imposed restraints on the part of teachers. Nonetheless, this component was approached with considerable awareness of and some experience with at least two of the remaining components. The goal commitments of the University Elementary School are stated in mankind terms, and there had been previous attempts to select subject matter with a mankind perspective. For example, a unit on the oceans had been used to explore how all humankind is affected by what happens to the sea around us. The implication is that whatever the specific focus of the project selected, there must be conscious effort to infuse all of the school's subject matter, culture, activities, and human relationships with mankind values and a mankind point of view.

Reflecting on our experience reveals that we had greatest difficulty with that which is most central—the very idea of mankind. Can it be taught? We were unable to wrap it up neatly with a precise label. It always eluded us just as we were about to encompass it. But is it that complex? Perhaps we were unable to recognize simplicity; we seemed to assume that it was not mankind if we could understand it. And yet we were unwilling to make of it a religion to be followed through faith alone. To seek always for understanding and thus to avoid cultism seemed to us imperative. At any rate, we decided that we did not yet know enough to teach mankind qua mankind and so attempted to infuse the whole of schooling with those aspects of mankind that fleetingly were revealed to us.

The Larger Context

Earlier, we commented on how difficult it is for schools to change. There usually is precious little support for change from the larger context of schooling. Whatever encouragement can be obtained from without simply is a bonus, a little "extra" to be drawn upon in time of unusual stress. The encouragement of someone higher in the administrative echelons means more to the success of a project than most such individuals seem to realize. Likewise, an informed and participating parent body can mean the difference between success and failure. In reflecting on our experience, we stress the importance of a school study group made up of children and parents as well as teachers and the principal. A representative from the office of the school district superintendent also would be helpful, especially for securing later support in the face of attack from or criticism by community groups or even colleagues from other schools.

It is doubtful, however, that a single school is strong enough to forge ahead on its own with a full-scale commitment to education for mankind and all this entails, known and unknown. Our studies of educational change have taught us the value of several schools joining in a common project for support, exchange of ideas, and mutual assistance.[8] Such a relationship must be taken seriously, however, with provision for meetings of principals on leadership problems, interschool committees, planned mechanisms for exchanging information, techniques for bringing together persons of like interests and problems, and so on. Taken seriously, the new relationships established can be sufficiently powerful to offset lack of support from the larger school enterprise and even criticism from a variety of sources. A league of cooperating schools joined for the purpose of each school working toward mankind educational goals could be a powerful mechanism for change.

It is for this reason that, as a follow-up of the project reported here, we have chosen to work with two consortia of schools committed to exploring the mankind idea. One, located in Southern California, provides an opportunity for a handful of schools, each in a different school district, to work closely together, exchanging ideas and materials as they proceed and gaining support from association with peers. This cluster of schools, in turn, belongs to an international consortium committed to common goals. The importance of this latter arrangement is assurance that the idea of mankind will be viewed from a variety of cultural backgrounds. The schools in this larger consortium are located in the major regions of the world and in countries varying in their religious orientations. The total number of schools represented in all of this is small, but taken together they provide a promising beachhead.

These networks are support systems. They provide simultaneously fresh ideas from outside the local school and an audience for one's own ideas and accomplishments. They provide encouragement during times of difficulty, sometimes making the difference between going on or giving up. Membership provides at least some of that important feeling of belonging to something larger than oneself—a tangible slice of mankind, if you will.

The Teacher's Role

But such support systems can only enhance, not take the place of, dedicated study, dialogue, and action of the kind summarized earlier—a process of attempting to understand and practice better what it means to conduct school from a mankind perspective. Ultimately, success will depend on teachers both as individuals and as teams. Some teachers will find the teaching behaviors called for to be radically different from their previous roles of telling, showing, or otherwise intervening in children's learning. Chapter 6 reveals vividly the self-discipline required by teachers: to behave consistently in rapidly changing, unpredictable circumstances; to resist children's demands for help which call for responses that would be inconsistent with the agreed-upon pedagogical purposes; to postpone gratification in efforts to achieve long-term rather than short-term goals. Good teaching is made up of so much more than interesting verbal performance. It is a composite of many little things, all related to a few central goals and principles. Full understanding of these basics and their implications for every aspect of schooling and pedagogy, together with the ability to stick with them hour after hour, day after day, is what marks the professional.

In effect, then, the teachers become models for the behavior sought in the children. They demonstrate—under fire, so to speak—their fundamental belief in the worth and dignity of each person and the ability of each child to become self-directing in disciplined ways. Children will test and test again to see if such beliefs are "for real." Do the teachers mean what they say about boys and girls making decisions for themselves, or is this just so much more of the verbiage they have heard time and time again? They test until, one by one, they become confident that the teachers will not, suddenly, do an about-face. It is a matter of trust.

Once the children realize that teachers are not likely to revert to stereotyped forms of "telling," of essentially taking away the opportunity to learn, they come face-to-face with a new and more formidable problem. It becomes their responsibility now to learn what is required in order to function as a decision-making body. Teachers, at all levels, usually are too impatient in working toward this critical point in learning. Some never try; they begin and end by telling passive learners. Information can be transmitted in this way, although this job, too, probably can be done better through books, television, or films. But if the goal is demonstrable behavior, a different pedagogy is called for. Guiding individuals to the point of realizing that the responsibility is theirs, that nobody else can or should be allowed to assume it, is a critical process. Done well, it is a joy to behold. The mankind school must be a crucible for this kind of becoming on the part of children and teachers alike.

A new unit in the curriculum or a new pedagogical procedure will not, by itself, change very much. Certainly, we will not proceed far toward a mankind school by inserting a little bit of process and substance here and there. But to infuse every aspect of the school with mankind goals, processes, content, and activities will make a difference. This uses the power of the school for the attainment of mankind goals.

As stated earlier, it is unrealistic to assume that the school alone can bring about a world fit for mankind. This is a problem for the whole of mankind. War, pollution, persecution, overpopulation, and like matters are mankind problems. They cannot be solved by individual states and nations. But schools are universal in the sense that they are scattered throughout the world, and they embrace more than 50 percent of the world's children. Where better to begin?

On Education for Mankind Consciousness

A wise man has said, "Mankind exists as a world society as soon as we become conscious of it." We have not as yet become conscious of mankind. It is to the creation of such consciousness that education can contribute.

We must be careful not to delude ourselves with misplaced faith in education. It can do little to solve those now-evident problems which cut across national interests and defy national capabilities to cope with them. These will be solved by creative, international engineering. But even to consider global engineering, let alone to tackle it, will require a measure of thinking in mankind terms. Such thinking is the product of education. Those frustratingly slow processes of education must go hand in hand, then, with those quicker human processes which employ only the fruits of education, processes designed to rectify those most immediately urgent global problems.

The hope for the long pull lies in education guided by a mankind perspective. Such education demands a new way of viewing old problems and hence will change the nature of these problems and the solutions they require. Education from such a perspective means developing a new morality. Things and actions become right or wrong, good or bad, to the extent that they support a unitary view of mankind. Education so guided leads to a new conception of human rights, cultivating a new conception of freedom. The freedom contemplated here brings together the basic ends of both the individual and mankind: to cultivate conditions which stimulate the full development of man's individual and collective potentials.

Education necessarily focuses on the individual. The individual tends to respond to surrounding contingencies which continuously reinforce him in daily life. Presently, these contingencies support parochial interests and behavior. To transcend these in order to encompass concern for a larger good is often considered divergent, deviant behavior which could lead to censure. The education required must produce, then, highly autonomous individuals, at least until there is a greater general consciousness of mankind.

Clearly, this mankind commitment will not come easily. It will not come to the narcissist preoccupied with self. It will not come to the hedonist living only for personal pleasure. It will not come to the now-oriented requiring immediate or early gratification. It will not come to the samaritan requiring immediate consequences from his good deeds, although he is on the way. It will not come to the academic who only reads and thinks. It will not come to the timid who must have a clear, safe course of action; there is not yet a flag or constitution, code or statute, to guide the way. For many, the mankind commitment simply will be too difficult.

The greatest hope, we think, lies with the young, with those in whom self-transcendence has had an early, sturdy beginning. Unfortunately, we know very little about the nature of this process and, consequently, about how to educate for it. Finding out more is a necessary inquiry. Ideally, self-transcendence matures throughout life, in the context of participating in mankind affairs. It is the function of education to prepare for and to enhance the reflective aspects of this participation.

This little volume seeks to make a small contribution to the necessary inquiry into education for self-transcendence and, ultimately, consciousness of mankind. It is addressed especially to that growing number of persons associated with schools who increasingly are anxious to fulfill the commitment they thought they were making when they entered teaching in the first place. We encourage school faculties everywhere, joined by children and parents, to think seriously about whether their schools are good places for children. This is a necessary first step, we think, toward a mankind school.

Notes

1. Reported in a series of books, I D E A *Reports on Schooling, Series on Educational Change,* McGraw-Hill Book Company, New York, 1973-1975.

2. David Cohen, "Why Curriculum Doesn't Matter," *New Leader,* vol. LIV, no. 22, Nov. 15, 1971, p. 7.

3. The findings are equivocal and controversial, the controversy surrounding the so-called Coleman Report being a case in point. See James S. Coleman et al., *Equality of Educational Opportunity,* U.S. Government Printing Office, Washington, D.C., 1966; and *Harvard Educational Review,* vol. 38, no. 1, Winter 1968.

4. See, for example, Ivan Illich, *Deschooling Society,* Harper & Row, Publishers, Incorporated, New York, 1971; and for the pro and con, Daniel U. Levine and Robert J. Havighurst (eds.), *Farewell to Schools?,* National Society for the Study of Education, Charles A. Jones Publishing Co., Worthington, Ohio, 1971.

5. For a comprehensive historical, sociological, and philosophical analysis of alternatives in education, see *New Directions for Education,* no. 4, Spring 1974.

6. Barbara Leondar, "The Counterschool Approach," *New Leader,* vol. LIV, no. 22, Nov. 15, 1971, pp. 14-15.

7. Our study of sixty-seven elementary schools revealed only a handful to have a staff even engaged in the effort. See John I. Goodlad, M. Frances Klein, and Associates, *Looking behind the Classroom Door,* rev. ed., Charles A. Jones Publishing Co., Worthington, Ohio, 1974.

8. Our experiences with such a strategy (not deliberately involving the mankind idea, however) are documented in a four-part film, *The League:* Part I, "The Strategy"; Part II, "A Matter of Trust"; Part III, "Try It Sometime"; Part IV, "I Just Wanted to Let You Know How Well Rhonda Is Doing in School." Film Reports on | I|D|E|A|'s Study of Change, Institute for Development of Educational Activities, Inc., An Affiliate of the Charles F. Kettering Foundation, Melbourne, Fla., 1971. The conduct and results of the study are described in Mary M. Bentzen and Associates, *Changing Schools: The Magic Feather Principle,* McGraw-Hill Book Company, New York, 1974.

Appendix
Mankind Workshop for Teachers

Course Outline Presented to Participants

The *expected outcomes* of this course will be an increased understanding of the dimensions of the mankind concept and an increased knowledge of resources available for developing a mankind curriculum. Participants also will be expected to begin analyzing their teaching from a mankind point of view with an eye to how the dimensions of mankind may be implemented in their own teaching.

The basic *content* of the course will be drawn from the attached framework, which has been developed for guiding the development of a mankind curriculum. The *methods* used will be extensive reading of pertinent publications dealing with aspects of the concept of mankind and of a mankind curriculum, attendance at lectures and discussions by consultants to the workshop, observation in the mankind project being taught at UES, and development and writing of an original rationale for a mankind curriculum.

The methods of evaluating the outcomes and objectives of the course will be through an instructor analysis of each student's contributions to discussions and lectures, and through each student's own analysis and synthesis of dimensions for a mankind curriculum (referred to in the above paragraph as an original rationale for a mankind curriculum).

Emphasis will be placed upon three *behavioral objectives:*

1. Comprehension of the concept of mankind.
2. Analysis of the critical dimensions and organizing elements of a mankind curriculum.
3. Synthesis of the critical dimensions of a mankind curriculum into a meaningful rationale.

Requirements of the course will include a critical review from each student of what he considers to be the essential dimensions of a mankind curriculum, a critical review of the tentative mankind framework with modification as gleaned from resources made available through the workshop, and a critique of the mankind curriculum taught at UES during this workshop.

There will be no required texts as such, but three publications are expected to be basic to the work of the participants:

1. Robert Ulich (ed.), *Education and the Idea of Mankind,* Harcourt, Brace & World, Inc., New York, 1964.
2. Louis E. Raths et al., *Values and Teaching: Working with Values in the Classroom,* Charles E. Merrill Books, Inc., Columbus, Ohio, 1966.
3. Publication in process on a mankind curriculum.

Tentative Schedule for Mankind Education Workshop

Monday, July 19

9 A.M.-12 P.M.	Introduction to and explanation of course. Observation: Evidence of humanism and mankind in classroom.
1 P.M.-3 P.M.	Discussion and summary of observations. Tentative identification of dimensions for mankind curriculum.
3 P.M.-5 P.M.	Library work.

Tuesday, July 20
9A.M.-12P.M.   Field trip to Wilmington School.
2P.M.-4P.M.   History of project.
                       Presentation of rationale and manuscript.
4P.M.-5P.M.   Library work.

Wednesday, July 21
9A.M.-12P.M.   Observation: Evidence of four dimensions in
                       rationale.
1P.M.-3P.M.   Panel of teachers on the mankind curriculum.

3P.M.-5P.M.   Library work.

Thursday, July 22
9A.M.-12P.M.   Observation: Focus on interaction.
1P.M.-3P.M.   Consultant: Topic, Humanism around the
                       World.
3P.M.-5P.M.   Library work.

Friday, July 23
9A.M.-11A.M.   Consultant
1P.M.-5P.M.   Library work.

Monday, July 26
9A.M.-10A.M.   Library work.
10A.M.-12P.M.   Consultant: Topic, Mankind and the *Geist* of
                       the School.
1P.M.-3P.M.   Consultant: Teachers and observers of the UES
                       summer program; topic, Documentation of the
                       Impact of the Curriculum.
3P.M.-5P.M.   Library work.

Tuesday, July 27
9A.M.-12P.M.   Observation: Focus on *Geist* of School.
1P.M.-3P.M.   Consultant: Panel of teachers; topic, An
                       Evolving Mankind Curriculum.
3P.M.-5P.M.   Library work.

Wednesday, July 28

9A.M.-12P.M.	Observation: Focus on subject matter.
1P.M.-3P.M.	Participants share lesson plans designed to illustrate the mankind concept.
3P.M.-5P.M.	Library work.

Thursday, July 29

9A.M.-12P.M.	Observation: Focus on three basic concepts.
1P.M.-4P.M.	Consultant: Topic, Mankind Education and Subject Matter.
4P.M.-5P.M.	Library work.

Friday, July 30

9A.M.-12P.M.	Observation: Focus on developmental levels of students.
1P.M.-5P.M.	Discussion of rationales.
	Feedback on workshop for instructors.

The Teacher Workshop: A Summary and Evaluation

A two-week summer workshop for teachers based on the concept of mankind was offered by Education Extension, UCLA, from July 19 to July 30, 1971. The class was scheduled from 9A.M. to 5P.M. for five days a week during the two-week period. The workshop granted four quarter hours of college credit to any participant who desired to earn them.

Education Extension of UCLA required a statement early in the spring regarding the expected outcomes, requirements of students, methods, and resources to be used and means of evaluation. The instructors of the workshop developed these requirements for Education Extension so that they were reflective of the interests and concerns of the project on mankind (see the course outline).

The backgrounds of the participants varied. They ranged from a principal of an elementary school who had her doctorate from UCLA and was very knowledgeable in the humanistic foundations of education to a young teacher who had taught for only one year at the primary level. There were several teachers at the primary level, one at the junior high level, and one at the high school level. One teacher worked with a group of gifted children and one with a team-taught multiaged group in an innovative school. Most were upper elementary school teachers with several years of experience.

The adult workshop was scheduled concurrently with the last two weeks of the children's summer session designed to implement a mankind curriculum. This allowed for observation of an ongoing program based on the rationale developed in the mankind project. Thus, the participants were involved in the ideas of mankind and in the rationale for implementing them while, at the same time, having an opportunity to observe how one group of teachers dealt with the concepts in practice.

An attempt was made to provide a balance of activities for the participants: observations, discussions, readings, consultants (both from the Council for the Study of Mankind and from the staff of the children's summer session), and projects, all of which were designed to lead the participants to inquire into the concept of mankind and into how it could be implemented in schools in general and in their own local situation specifically. Seven of the ten mornings were spent observing the children engaged in the activities of a mankind curriculum. The participants were asked to focus on specific parts of the rationale each time they observed. Time was allowed at the beginning of each afternoon session for questions, comments, or analyses of what had been observed in the morning. In addition, on several occasions, the staff working with the children joined the adult workshop to explain their approach to a mankind curriculum and to engage in the general discussions of the group. These sessions with the staff of the children's workshop proved to be very meaningful for all participants.

Several consultants were brought in to lead discussions. Analyses centered on the concept of mankind, the rationale, or the humanistic approach to education. Two films helped to illustrate the type of interaction and school climate which a mankind curriculum would require. Much reading material was made available and used extensively. Many of the references listed in the bibliography were provided.

Each participant was asked to develop a project to illustrate how the concept of mankind could be introduced into the back-home teaching situation. Some of these projects were discussed in class. Each participant was asked to prepare a critique of the rationale, paying particular attention to its strengths, limitations, and practicality. Suggestions for modification were also solicited.

The results of the assignment were varied. For example, a beginning teacher described her tentative program for young children who would be starting school in Nairobi, Kenya. Her program was designed to help children know themselves—a beginning step toward a mankind perspective. Two teachers developed an instrument which attempted to assess how the children engaged in the mankind program felt about the summer school as contrasted with their regular school. Themes which often appeared in the children's answers cited appreciation of the freedom and alternatives provided in the summer school and for the relaxed, open, and honest way in which the teachers interacted with them. Another teacher wrote a very thoughtful analysis of her understanding of the concept of mankind. Common to all the projects and critiques was evidence of a sincere effort to understand what is meant by mankind and to incorporate this understanding into individual school settings.

The two instructors of the workshop were encouraged from the first day by the levels of insight and interest which the participants displayed. Difficulties had been anticipated. For example, the instructors considered the course content to be at a rather high level of abstraction. It was apparent, however, that the participants were "in tune" with the content, beginning immediately to explore the meaning of mankind and ways through which it could be made a part of schooling. Many indicated, though, that mankind was an elusive, complex concept which they had difficulty understanding. It is likely that all participants had some initial interest in the humanistic processes of education, or they would not have been willing to spend their time, effort, and money on such a workshop. Therefore, most or all probably were favorably inclined toward many of the ideas at the outset. Clearly, initial interests and understanding were sharpened and deepened as the workshop progressed.

Throughout the workshop, learning opportunities were chosen or designed to reflect the spirit of inquiry which characterized the entire project. The rationale was presented as only a tentative formulation, that is, as one way to help students achieve a mankind perspective. Alternatives, limitations, strengths, and modifications were sought constantly. This spirit of inquiry was accepted quite readily by most participants, but occasionally someone would try to push for definitive answers or "recipes" for solution of the problems being raised. In these instances, the instructors reiterated that the project was a search guided by a few key concepts but without predetermined solutions. Participants were encouraged to formulate their own positions on all issues.

The final morning of the workshop was set aside for summative evaluation. In general, the reactions of participants were positive and enthusiastic about both the content of the project and the conduct of the workshop. Formidable difficulties were seen by some of the participants in introducing the ideas discussed into conservative, traditional school systems. At the end of the workshop, however, each participant appeared to have identified beginning points to implement some of the concepts pertinent to the idea of mankind and to the rationale of the project. The instructors were convinced by the workshop experience that the mankind concepts could be grasped by the average teacher and translated into school and classroom practice.

Toward a Mankind School
Annotated Bibliography
Lillian K. Drag

PART I: EDUCATION FOR MANKIND

This limited listing may be amply supplemented by the bibliographies which appear in many of the Council for the Study of Mankind publications. Especially helpful is the bibliography in *A Record of Activities,* Council for the Study of Mankind, Inc., Chicago, 1962, pp. 53-63.

Agel, Jerome: *Is Today Tomorrow: A Synergistic Collage of Alternative Futures,* Ballantine Books, Inc., New York, 1972.
The dangers and promises of technology are visually and verbally portrayed in the context of the future—and the world.

Beck, C. M., B. S. Crittenden, and E. V. Sullivan (eds.): *Moral Education: Interdisciplinary Approaches,* University of Toronto Press, Toronto, 1971.
More questions are raised than answered in this report of a conference held June 1968 at the Ontario Institute for Studies in Education. Nevertheless, the qualified philosophers, sociologists, psychologists, and educators offer their best thinking on the conflicts and perplexities over the meaning of morality.

Boulding, Kenneth E.: "The Interplay of Technology and Values: The Emerging Superculture," in Kurt Baier and Nicholas Rescher (eds.), *Values and the Future,* The Free Press, New York, 1969.
Sees the major problems of the world revolving around the tensions between the "superculture" and the various old national, religious, ethnic, etc., cultures.

Brameld, Theodore: *The Climactic Decades, Mandate to Education,* Frederick A. Praeger, Inc., New York, 1970.
Foreword by K. Benne: "One overarching purpose of education—the purpose of a converging humanity engaged in ever-restless, ever-anxious search for its own ultimate meaning and its own deepest fulfillment." His message is a vision of a future-centered education, alive and open to the threats and promises of a technological civilization which has lost its human bearings, committed to building processes of personal and cultural renewal into the fabric of an emerging world society.
Chapter 2: "Imperatives for a Future-centered Education."
Chapter 3: "Experimental Centers for the Creation of World Civilization."
Chapter 6: "Confronting the Values of Youth."
Appendix: "Reconstructionism," pp. 195-200, a pragmatic, experimentalist position in American philosophy.

Bronowski, Jacob: *The Identity of Man,* The National History Press, Garden City, N.Y., 1965.
Enlarges upon the theme developed in *Science and Human Values* to examine "the fields over which the imaginative mind ranges: in the act of discovery in science and the act of creation in the arts." Seeks to discover unity.

Cantril, Hadley, and C.H. Bumstead: *Reflections on the Human Venture,* New York University Press, New York, 1960.
Excerpts from poems, plays, prayers, and other writings are used to exemplify man's relation to man and to the universe.

Chase, Stuart: *The Most Probable World,* Penguin Books, Inc., Baltimore, 1969. Clear, concise writing and thought-provoking ideas with descriptions and examples enhance the discussions of "The Arms Race," "Nationalism—Which Way," and "One World." The last chapter is on the year 2000.

deVries, Egbert: "The Image of Mankind," mimeographed paper, Council for the Study of Mankind, Inc., no date.
Traces how the concept of mankind has enlarged and grown through history. Identifies why we need a new concern and commitment to our development and understanding of it. Emphasizes concepts of diversity and reciprocity in the idea of mankind. Also identifies some unifying thoughts within our world leading toward the concept of mankind. Suggests the value of the image of mankind serving a needed purpose of inspiration.

Drews, Elizabeth Monroe, and Leslie Lipson: *Values and Humanity,* St. Martin's Press, Inc., New York, 1971.
What is the nature of man? "As human beings, we are what we value." Believing that values have to be ranked in a hierarchy in order to endow "human life with a standard for decision-making," the authors argue that three characteristics are fundamental to humanity: "the need to choose, our subjective awareness that we are choosing, and our need to choose well." They feel it is necessary to discuss what we should value if we are to become more fully human. Biological, psychological, and anthropological bases for a universal hierarchy of values are presented, as are the ethical and aesthetic bases. In detailing stages of individual development, the highest stage, Level VII: World Man, Universal Man, etc., is the one we are striving for. Discussions of the assertion of the self, the love of community, the quest for a universal society, and the virtue of the small community are pertinent.

Dubos, René: *So Human an Animal,* Charles Scribner's Sons, New York, 1968.
A readable and important book designed to illustrate that each individual is unique in the ways his person responds to his environment; that all experiences leave their mark, especially very early influences; that "human beings are as much the product of their total environment as of their genetic endowment." The author sees the present system on a suicidal course which can be averted with a science of human life. "Man makes himself through enlightened choices that enhance his humanness."

Erikson, Erik H.: *Childhood and Society,* 2d ed. (rev. and enl.), W. W. Norton & Company, Inc., New York, 1963.
Chapter 7, "Eight Ages of Man," contributes a developmental framework which may be useful in curriculum construction. See Richard Jones, *Fantasy and Feeling in Education,* New York University Press, New York, 1968, for an example of its use.

Fairfield, Roy P. (ed.): *Humanistic Frontiers in American Education,* Prentice-Hall, Inc., Englewood Cliffs, N.J., 1971.
A most pertinent collection of essays for expanding and deepening one's understanding of the mankind concept. Listed below are brief annotations of a

few of these provocative essays: Theodore Brameld, "Illusions and Disillusions in American Education," pp. 17-27; urges action in dealing with present crises, examining critically the illusions and realities in American education—among which is the illusion of nationalism. His solution: "The problems and expectations of all mankind should become nothing less than the pervading theme of *every* curriculum, beginning in its own terms of maturation at the kindergarten level and extending to college and adult levels." Roy P. Fairfield, "A Teacher as Radical Humanist," pp. 237-247; delves into the teacher-student relationship, viewing it in its ethical aspects—a description of personal humanism in action. Jack L. Nelson, "Nationalistic Education and the Free Man," pp. 139-147; proposes a new definition for nationalistic education which would make it in the national interest to develop free men through open inquiry and the presumption of change, permitting challenges to prevalent national values, and not demanding unquestioning acceptance. Robert Theobald and Noel McInnis, "A Certain Education for an Uncertain Time"; propose a fresh start, examining the true meaning of education in a cybernated era—"What do we mean by the process of socialization for a world in which toil is unnecessary?" Challenge third-hand experience about the nature of the world, espousing true dialogue. Benjamin F. Thompson, "Education: The Most Dangerous Game," pp. 312-314; believing that the major responsibility of education is to test whether freedom will work and, secondly, that the "how" of education is more important than the "what," Thompson plays the game "Twenty-five Questions."

Falk, Richard A.: *This Endangered Planet: Prospects and Proposals for Human Survival,* Random House, Inc., New York, 1971.
Analyzes the four principal dangers: the war system, overpopulation, the depletion of natural resources, and the deterioration of the entire environment. Then considers the philosophical, political, and economic changes that are needed to avert disaster.

Feinberg, Gerald: *The Prometheus Project: Mankind's Search for Long-range Goals,* Doubleday & Company, Inc., Garden City, N.Y., 1969.
The stated purpose of the book is to convince as many people as possible of the need for long-range goals. Suggests a systematic plan of discussion, giving examples of global goal setting. A mind-expanding and thought-extending treatise, directly related to mankind concepts.

Freire, Paulo: *Pedagogy of the Oppressed,* Myra Bergman Ramos (trans.), Herder and Herder, Inc., New York, 1970.
One of the educational revolutionaries who argues that formal schooling is inherently oppressive. "This movement of inquiry must be directed towards humanization— man's historical vocation. The pursuit of full humanity, however, cannot be carried out in isolation or individualization, but only in fellowship and solidarity." Emphasizes dialogue, the continuous interaction between students and teachers.

Fromm, Erich: *The Revolution of Hope,* Harper & Row, Publishers, Incorporated, New York, 1968.
Chapter IV ("What Does It Mean to Be Human?") provides basic understandings of human nature and its various manifestations; the conditions of human existence;

orientation, survival, and transsurvival needs; an array of "humane experiences"; and values and norms.

Gaevernitz, Ruth V. S.: *Aristotle, Alexander and the Idea of Mankind,* mimeographed paper. Council for the Study of Mankind, Inc., no date.
Reports the beginning of the idea of mankind from the works and records of the ancient Greeks.

Gardner, John: *Self-Renewal: The Individual and the Innovative Society,* Harper & Row, Publishers, Incorporated, New York, 1963.
Recognizes the need for a commitment to some ultimate ideal and values: "But embarrassment about the expression of moral seriousness is a disease of people far gone in affectation and oversophistication; unaffected people will regard it as normal to consult their deepest values and to exhibit allegiance to those values," p. 21.

Goodlad, John I.: "Education for Mankind," *International Understanding at School,* UNESCO, no. 26, November 1973, pp. 3-5.
Describes the attempt to initiate action in furthering the idea of mankind in schools throughout the world, pinpointing initial efforts made here. Discusses projected plans for continuing such efforts.

————: "Mankind and International Education," *The UCLA Educator,* vol. 14, Spring 1972, pp. 3-6.
Delineates the concept of mankind and basic assumptions upon which school programs may be developed.

———— and Associates: *Toward a Mankind School: An Adventure in Humanistic Education,* manuscript, Council for the Study of Mankind, Inc., and Educational Inquiry, Inc., Los Angeles, 1971.
A report to the Ford Foundation describing the beginning of a search to explore the concept of mankind with ideas about mankind, their significance for teachers and children, and their relationship to the culture of the school. Attempts to translate these ideas into a curriculum for children.

Goodman, Mary Ellen: *The Individual and Culture,* The Dorsey Press. Homewood, Ill., 1967.
Examines the interrelationship between the nature and means of human development and the nature and impact of culture on the individual. Presents basic concepts dealing with individual autonomy versus cultural determinism as used by anthropologists and sociologists.

Hall, Edward J.: *The Silent Language,* Doubleday & Company, Inc., Garden City, N.Y., 1959.
Develops the concept of cultural universalism, supporting the view that both human qualities and human culture are "universal." Proposes a theory with colleague George Traeger, based on the conviction that culture is communication and communication is culture. Identifies ten kinds of basic human activities (Primary Message Systems) based on anthropological studies. See also his *The Hidden Dimension,* Doubleday & Company, Inc., Garden City, N.Y., 1969.

Hampden-Turner, Charles: *Radical Man: The Processes of Psycho-Social Develop-

ment, Schenkman Publishing Co., Inc., Cambridge, Mass., 1970.
Develops a model of psychosocial development which he finds parallels Kohlberg's moral stages. Argues that only a human concern which is translated into principled action can maintain our mental and social integration.

Harman, Willis W.: "Policies for National Reunification," *Journal of Creative Behavior,* vol. 4, Fall 1970, pp. 283-293.
Presents six propositions (hypotheses) relating to the present state of society and the probable future course of events. Basic premises of "New Age" culture include an image of man as a part of a Whole and contain the "communion with nature prerequisite to resolving the planet's ecological problems, the fraternity to fellow man without which social problems will resist solution, and the supremely meaningful task of human evolution to eliminate the anomie of our time."

Hill, Christopher (ed.): *Rights and Wrongs: Essays on Human Rights,* Penguin Books, Inc., Baltimore, 1969.
Case histories reveal disregard for human rights. Discusses philosophical principles underlying the question of human rights and reviews international organizations involved in redressing human wrongs.

Hines, Paul D., and Leslie Wood: *A Guide to Human Rights Education,* National Council for the Social Studies, Washington, D.C., 1969.
Contains a wealth of resource information on the progress of human rights up to the present. Includes the Universal Declaration of Human Rights, the Human Rights Creed on Education, the Declaration of the Rights of the Child, and other human rights documents in the appendix.

Hirschfeld, Gerhard: *An Essay on Mankind,* Philosophical Library, Inc., New York, 1967.
Suggests some ways by which the concept of mankind may become better defined, largely in opposition to other groups which now possess different purposes and plans. Analyzes contemporary thought to look for evidence of the mankind concept without much success. Examines several institutions to understand why they have not contributed more to the development of mankind: education, science, religion, and art. Gives suggestions for further development of the concept in the future.

————: "The Idea of Mankind: A New and Vital Instrument," mimeographed paper, address presented to the National Council for the Social Studies, Nov. 30, 1963, Council for the Study of Mankind, Inc.
This short paper discusses three aspects of the meaning of the concept of mankind for the world today. Although mankind is an old concept, it is not well understood by most people. We must begin developing an understanding of and a commitment to mankind if we are to survive. Some problems encountered in doing this are identified.

————: *The People: Growth and Survival, First Cycle,* Aldine Publishing Company, Chicago, 1973.
Defines "the people" and attempts to explain why they "have never attained lasting freedom, security, and self-determination—briefly, dignity." Makes specific proposals for the creation of a mankind-oriented society. Invites response from readers, pro and con. A challenging, understandable, and readable treatise.

————: "Teachers Should Understand Mankind," *Teachers College Record,* vol. 70, March 1969, pp. 541-548.
Suggests urgency to understand the concept of mankind in our world today. An inadequate framework of viewing the world and problems seen from segmental viewpoints are a major block in understanding mankind. Children may be exempt from this block. Gives suggestions about how topics may be viewed differently from these two perspectives. Education must assist in transcending segmental views and interpretations, in thinking and evaluating in a mankind framework, and in developing programs which develop understanding of and commitment to mankind.

Hoffman, Paul G.: *The Future of Mankind in a Shrinking World,* mimeographed paper, address delivered to the Council for the Study of Mankind, Inc., Nov. 7, 1963.
Describes some conditions of the world that imperil the future of mankind. Outlines several projects which the Special Fund of the United Nations is directing to improve the lot of some people in underdeveloped nations and, it is hoped, the future of mankind. Also, describes the magnitude of the task of preparing underdeveloped nations to help themselves, but concludes that it is a reasonable task which can be accomplished in this century.

Hoselitz, Bert F. (ed.): *Economics and the Idea of Mankind,* Columbia University Press, New York, 1965.
Erskine McKinley, "Mankind in the History of Economic Thought," Chapter 1, introduces the concept of mankind. Then the book attempts to clarify two questions: What are the chief characteristics of an economy embracing all mankind; and what measures may be taken to bring the world closer to such a result?

Klein, M. Frances, Jerrold M. Novotney, and Kenneth A. Tye: "A Mankind Perspective: New Charge for the Social Studies," *Childhood Education,* vol. 49, October 1972, pp. 3-8.
Reports a study designed to conceptualize a rationale for including the mankind view as a goal of schooling. Describes the attempt to develop an approach to it in schools, using the experienced teachers at the University Elementary School, UCLA, to implement some of the basic ideas in a summer workshop.

Kluckhohn, Clyde: *Mirror for Man,* Premier Books, Fawcett World Library, New York, 1970.
Highly recommended classic cultural anthropology text now available in paperback edition.

Launching Operation Man to Mankind: Toward Grass-roots Involvement in Designing the Global Democracy of the 21st Century, Southern Connecticut State College, Center for Interdisciplinary Creativity, New Haven, Conn. 06515, 1971.
An interim report on the international workshop, Conceptual and Attitudinal Pathways from Man to Mankind, sponsored by the Alvin K. Kazanjian Economics Foundation. Seems to parallel our efforts at developing a mankind view, though intent on employing general systems analysis.

Lyford, Joseph: "Education and World Affairs," *Intercultural Education,* June-July 1970, pp. 1-2, 27.

Brief outline of major problems facing mankind. Deals with possible solutions by educational institutions and services.

Macdonald, James B., Bernice J. Wolfson, and Esther Zaret: *Reschooling Society: A Conceptual Model,* Association for Supervision and Curriculum Development, Washington, D.C., 1973..
Provides a much-needed theoretical base for person-oriented schools (and mankind schools) by restructuring the sociocultural, psychological, and transactional dimensions of schooling. Sociological dimensions of liberation, pluralism, and participation are particularly apt for a mankind program. Psychologically, the creation of "personal meaning through acting upon and transforming tentative patterns of knowing into personal knowledge" is stressed as well as "higher levels of self-esteem, commitment, responsibility, freedom, and an ever-expanding awareness of the world."

Mead, Margaret: *Culture and Commitment: A Study of the Generation Gap,* Doubleday & Company, Garden City, N.Y., 1970.
The author provides an understanding of cultural character and offers some of the measures she thinks need to be taken in "applying our growing understanding of culture to man's precarious situation." Believing that we are on the verge of developing a new kind of culture, the author proposes the "care and feeding" of a new breed of human beings, nurtured to develop independently of the past, free to grow and discover new "ways of teaching and learning that will keep the future open." "We must create new models for adults who can teach their children not what to learn, but how to learn and not what they should be committed to, but the value of commitment."

————: *Family,* photographs by Ken Heyman, Collier Books, The Macmillan Company, New York, 1971.
Pictures taken in over forty countries carry text by Dr. Mead on human roles and relationships.

Myers, Donald A.: "The Humanistic School: A Critical Analysis," *The Educational Forum,* vol. 37, November 1972, pp. 53-58.
Describes the development of ideas while involved with the mankind curriculum at the UCLA University Elementary School under the direction of John I. Goodlad.

Phenix, Philip H.: *Realms of Meaning: A Philosophy of the Curriculum for General Education,* McGraw-Hill Book Company, New York, 1964.
Based on "a concept of human nature as rooted in meaning and of human life as directed toward the fulfillment of meaning." Effective realization of essential humanness through the curriculum of general education. Realms four and five deal with personal knowledge and ethics or moral knowledge. Realm six, synoptics, refers to meanings that are comprehensively integrative: history, religion, and philosophy, which combine meaning into coherent wholes.

Polak, Fred: *The Images of the Future,* Elise Boulding (trans. and abridger), Jossey-Bass, Inc., San Francisco, 1973.
A difficult conceptual work, attempting to clarify "the role of the image of the future in the social process at the societal level." Provides a look at the broad sweep of the underlying historical processes leading to the impending "common

global heritage on earth." A deep and thoughtful treatise, philosophically and intellectually.

Rich, John Martin: *Humanistic Foundations of Education,* Charles A. Jones Publishing Co., Worthington, Ohio, 1971.

Chapter 1, "The Question of Man," outlines briefly the thinking of leading philosophers, such as Pierre Teilhard de Chardin, Illich, and the humanistic psychologists and existentialists. Chapter 2, "The Student as a Person," includes a discussion of Martin Buber's *I and Thou.*

The Study of Mankind, excerpts from the publications of the Council for the Study of Mankind, Inc.

Summarizes major ideas from seven conferences held under the auspices of the Council and from two books published under the auspices of the Council. A few ideas help in developing the concept of mankind; more are related to subject matter than to mankind. Indicates range of concern and involvement of the Council in developing the concept of mankind.

Taylor, Harold: *The World and the American Teacher: The Preparation of Teachers in the Field of World Affairs,* The American Association of Colleges for Teacher Education, 1968.

An AACTE study of the problems and possibilities of extending the education of teachers into an international dimension so that they acquire an international point of view and the knowledge to go with it. Develops ideas for using the entire culture as an instrument of education, taking account of the fact that an understanding of the world at large depends for its accomplishment on a prior understanding of oneself in relation to one's own society.

Thompson, Laura: *Toward a Science of Mankind,* McGraw-Hill Book Company, New York, 1961.

For an understanding of the concept of mankind see p. 136.

Ulich, Robert: "Higher Education and the Future of Mankind," mimeographed paper, address presented to the 16th National Conference on Higher Education, Mar. 7, 1961, Council for the Study of Mankind, Inc.

Discusses obligations of higher education to mankind, but much is applicable to any level of schooling. Discusses ways in which education can contribute to the role of the growing person in our society. Suggests some qualities of a person which would seem to be important in developing a mankind perspective and commitment to mankind.

——— (ed.): *Education and the Idea of Mankind,* Harcourt, Brace & World, Inc., New York, 1964.

This book is probably the most definitive single source for a mankind curriculum. Ulich, in his chapter, discusses self-transcendence; Biber, Goodlad, and Johnson discuss how aspects of the mankind concept might be implemented in schools.

———: "The Person and Organizations," Arthur Kroll (ed.), in *Issues in American Education,* Oxford University Press, New York, 1970, pp. 184-202.

Discusses six interrelated concepts: I, ego, individual, self, person, and mankind or humanity. A philosophical view of the interdependence of the person with the world of organizations.

UNESCO, International Commission on the Development of Education: *Learning To Be: The World of Education Today and Tomorrow,* Edgar Faure (chairman), UNESCO, Paris; George G. Harrap & Co., Ltd., London, 1972.

Report of the year-long "critical reflection by men of different origins and backgrounds seeking...for over-all solutions to the major problems involved in the development of education in a changing universe." Faure's preamble offers the rationale for a mankind point of view: "The new man must be capable of understanding the global consequences of individual behavior, of conceiving of priorities, and shouldering his share of the joint responsibility involved in the destiny of the human race." Chapter 8, "Elements for Contemporary Strategies," indicates the range of improvement and reforms and gives principles, considerations, recommendations, and illustrations of specific innovations from various countries.

Views and Ideas of Mankind, bulletins of the Council for the Study of Mankind, Inc., published periodically.

Bulletin 26, July 1970, contains articles by Krader on ecology and the threat to man for lack of adequate water supply, and by Platt on what might be done through social intervention to deal with crisis problems of man today. Also contains letters from various parts of the world dealing with the concept of mankind and brief reports on projects under the auspices of the Council.

Bulletin 27 has similar content with articles by Alisjahbana suggesting four levels of understanding people of different backgrounds, by Anees on his view of man and his world, by Boulding on the future and various images of it, and by Charlier and Schwartz on the development of cities.

Wagar, W. Warren: *Building the City of Man: Outlines of a World Civilization,* Grossman Pub., New York, 1971.

Builds an image of the future and describes specific strategies for making the image a reality. Chapter 6, "Education," discusses work as growth; learning in and out of the educational establishment, centered on the person; schools and values; the free academy; and cognitive synthesis (the integration of human knowledge).

———— (ed.): *History and the Idea of Mankind,* The University of New Mexico Press, Albuquerque, 1971.

The first five chapters trace the idea of mankind in five historic cultures: Indian, Chinese, Jewish, Muslim, and Helleno-Christian. The last four chapters deal with the modern world: nationalism and internationalism, science and technology, race, and religion.

Wallia, C. S. (ed.): *Toward Century 21,* Basic Books, Inc., Publishers, New York, 1970.

Presents a readable and frequently disturbing synthesis of technology, social change, and human values, with a bearing on decisions regarding a "good" world for tomorrow. Distinguished authorship.

Wright, Quincy: "Toward a Universal Law for Mankind," *Columbia Law Review,*

vol. 63, March 1963, pp. 435-458.
Identifies some basic issues to be considered if the concept of mankind is to govern laws and rule of nations. The issues have broader applicability than just to law and politics. Traces concern for universal law in past history and cites present conditions which point to the need for a universal law for mankind.

PART II: THE CULTURE OF THE SCHOOL

Childhood Education, vol. 49, no. 5, February 1973, Association for Childhood Education International, Washington, D.C.
The theme of this issue, "Helping Children with Conflict Resolution," treats school climate, teaching, and children's attitudes with a position paper, "Children and War." Many helpful suggestions and materials are included.

Cogswell, John F.: "Humanistic Approaches to the Design of Schools," A. M. Kroll (ed.), in *Issues in American Education: Commentary on the Current Scene,* Oxford University Press, New York, 1970, pp. 98-117.
Questions the assumptions underlying the traditional systems approach as it applies to education. Presents a rationale for developing humanistic procedures for the development of schools.

Crary, Ryland W.: *Humanizing the School,* Alfred A. Knopf, Inc., New York, 1969.
Implications for a mankind curriculum are scattered throughout the book. Particularly helpful are sections "With a View of Man," pp. 51-74, and Part III, "Learning Resources and the Human Potential." There will probably be much to agree with and much to disagree with as the author presents his ideas on what is currently wrong with the schools and what is needed to make them more humanistic.

Culver, Carmen M., and Gary J. Hoban (eds.): *The Power to Change: Issues for the Innovative Educator,* McGraw-Hill Book Company, New York, 1973.
Report of a five-year study by the |I|D|E|A| Research Division, focusing on "the single school as the theatre for change." Deals, in part, with the power of the elementary school principal, stages of change in the schools, criteria for a good school, and the peer group strategy for effecting change.

Engel, Martin: "The Humanities and the Schools," *Teachers College Record,* vol. 72, December 1970, pp. 239-248.
The author calls for humanization of the school and, in so doing, denounces the *Geist* of the school as he sees it. Also, there are some implications for the type of person desired by those who want humanization of education to occur.

Fox, Robert S., and Ronald Lippitt: *The Human Relations School,* mimeographed paper, University of Michigan, Center for Research Utilization of Scientific Knowledge, 1968.
A model prepared at the request of CFK, Ltd., of a school program which focused on inquiry into human relations based on specific assumptions from which goals are derived. Goals are spelled out and strategies for implementation suggested.

Examples: "Goal Area 5: Open and Supportive Climate" and "Goal Area 6: Human Relations in the Classroom."

Fox, Robert S., and Others: *School Climate Improvement: A Challenge to the School Administrator,* CFK, Ltd., Englewood, Colo., 1973 (field test version).
Delineate school climate factors: respect, trust, high morale, caring, and others. Develop a profile based on them to aid the administrator rate his school's climate. Make suggestions for initiating climate improvement and describe activities for furthering improvement.

Fox, Robert S., Ronald Lippitt, and Eva Schindler-Rainman: *Toward a Humane Society: Images of Potentiality,* Learning Resources Corporation, Fairfax, Va., 1973.
Three case studies build illustrative images of what a more humanizing society could be like: (1) "The Socializing Community," (2) "The Humanizing School," and (3) "The Volunteering Community." Case 2 describes the educational goal of achieving sensitivity and competence in humaneness. Stresses creation of a supportive ecology and maintenance of open and supportive communication.

Fuchs, Estelle: *Teachers Talk: Views from inside City Schools,* Doubleday & Company, Inc., Garden City, N.Y., 1969.
Shows what the school does to beginning teachers, focusing on their problems and pressures for conforming to the institution. Provides any teacher with an awareness of possibilities for changing the system.

Goodlad, John I., M. Frances Klein, and Associates: *Behind the Classroom Door,* Charles A. Jones Publishing Co., Worthington, Ohio, 1970.
A devastating revelation of the present school situation based on close scrutiny by a team of experienced teachers. The study includes a careful analysis which serves as the basis for recommendations in order to develop a more humane, effective, and satisfying environment for learning.

————: *Looking behind the Classroom Door: A Useful Guide to Observing Schools in Action,* Charles A. Jones Publishing Co., Worthington, Ohio, 1974.
A revised edition of the previous title with added emphasis on the process of observing life in schools, especially by teams of pre-service or in-service teachers, change agents, and researchers.

International Understanding at School, UNESCO, Paris, 1965.
On the UNESCO Associated Schools Project which emphasized the importance of the atmosphere of the school in which all members of that "community" are treated equally. "The principles of human rights should be reflected in the organization and conduct of school life, in classroom methods, and in relations between teachers and students and among teachers themselves."

Jackson, Philip W.: *Life in Classrooms,* Holt, Rinehart and Winston, Inc., New York, 1968.
Closely examines the school as a setting for human activity and finds there is much left to be desired in the learning environment provided for children. See also his *The Teacher and the Machine,* The University of Pittsburgh Press, Pittsburgh, 1967.

Macdonald, James B., Bernice J. Wolfson, and Esther Zaret: *Reschooling Society: A Conceptual Model,* Association for Supervision and Curriculum Development, Washington, D.C., 1973.
The transactional dimensions of the theoretical model suggest a humanistic educational environment; a teacher-student relationship of mutual respect and trust; and curriculum "as environment" to encompass political, social, personal, and cultural actions (creation of new cultural meanings).

Pritzkau, Philo: *The Dynamics of Curriculum Improvement,* Prentice-Hall, Inc., Englewood Cliffs, N.J., 1959.
Describes a total values admission classroom as one in which all values are admitted for consideration and analysis. The teacher and the learner involve themselves in the dynamics of the collective existence of ideas and values, and alternatives are considered.

Rogers, Carl: *Freedom to Learn,* Charles E. Merrill Books, Inc., Columbus, Ohio, 1969.
Rogers assembles here his thoughts about the learning process in education with specific examples at three different levels of education. He presents some of the assumptions upon which this approach is based, including the problems of values and the meaning of freedom in today's world. As in *On Becoming a Person,* he gives a personal view of what it means to live in relationship with one's fellow man.

Rubin, Louis J., and Others: *Facts and Feelings in the Classroom,* Walker and Co., New York, 1973.
Eight leaders of educational change contribute articles relating to the need for a new kind of curriculum involving children's feelings. They propose that the school must concern itself with more than cognition—feeling, thinking, and valuing are equally important concerns. Benjamin Bloom, Abraham Maslow, Richard Jones, Elliot Eisner, Ralph Tyler, Edward Meade, Jr., and Michael Scriven as well as Rubin look at the school environment, the society, the teacher, and the child and his feelings in the instructional process.

Sarason, Seymour B.: *Creation of Settings and Future Societies,* Jossey-Bass, Inc., San Francisco, 1972.
Examines the processes and problems common to the creation of settings ("any instance where two or more people come together in new and sustained relationships"). Draws upon personal participation in the creation of new settings in education and other fields to describe and analyze failures and successes. Social systems, socialization, and leadership are examined.

————: *The Culture of the School and the Problem of Change,* Allyn and Bacon, Inc., Boston, 1971.
The author chose to experience the school culture through the "helping relationship." Looks at what exists in school and why and what alternative ways of thinking might change the way things are. The ecological approach to the description of schooling gives deeper insights into what is going on that needs changing.

Saylor, J. Galen, and Joshua L. Smith (eds.): *Removing Barriers to Humaneness in the High School,* Association for Supervision and Curriculum Development, Washington, D.C., 1971.

A position paper presented by James B. Macdonald, "A Vision of a Humane School," is examined and evaluated by other conferees. They identify some major barriers and discuss ways in which schools could "break out of the box." James Foley's "Teaching and Learning in the Affective Domain" describes teaching techniques used to create conditions of mutual respect and cooperativeness. Fred Wilhelms designs a curriculum.

To Nurture Humaneness: Commitment for the '70's, 1970 Yearbook, Association for Supervision and Curriculum Development, Washington, D.C., 1970.

Part I offers a variety of statements on perceptions of humanness and humaneness. Part III, "Inhibiting and Facilitating Forces in Nurturing Humaneness," discusses forces in the school setting which affect development of humane capabilities. The final section describes school practices, good and bad, which may help or hinder humaneness. No specific curriculum is presented, but the foundation upon which curriculum might be based is proposed.

The Unstudied Curriculum: Its Impact on Children, Association for Supervision and Curriculum Development, Washington, D.C., 1970.

Lawrence Kohlberg, in "The Moral Atmosphere of the School," pp. 104-127, discusses the "need to make the hidden curriculum an atmosphere of justice and to make it explicit in intellectual and verbal discussion of justice and morale." Universal civil rights and support of the universal sacredness of human life are issues in which the most morally mature students are most active. Appends Table I, "Definition of Moral Stages"; six stages—from the preoperational level to the universal ethical principle orientation.

Williams, Richard C., et al.: *Effecting Organizational Renewal in Schools: A Social Systems Perspective,* McGraw-Hill Book Company, New York, 1974.

Based on a research study conducted by the I|D|E|A Research Division, inquiring into the reasons for attainment of a school's goals. It describes the relationship between the social system of the school and its ability to effect change. Leadership, role-personality conflict, and value orientation were studied. Findings stressed the complexity of introducing change into schools and indicated those factors which hindered or promoted attempted changes.

PART III: HUMAN RELATIONS IN A MANKIND SCHOOL

Ashton-Warner, Sylvia: *Teacher,* Simon & Schuster, Inc., New York, 1963.

Still one of the best sources for portraying the humanistic teacher interacting with her students, relating the student's own concerns and life-styles to his learning. She allows children to generate content out of their own needs and experiences but guides them into understanding the broad implications of their personal concerns.

Baier, Kurt, and Nicholas Rescher: *Values and the Future,* The Free Press, New York, 1969.
Provide a means for analyzing values in order to choose them, introducing the idea of "Value Domain," the boundaries of a value. Relate the importance of values in determining the quality of life in the future.

Barr, Robert D. (ed.): *Values and Youth: Teaching Social Studies in an Age of Crisis—No. 2,* National Council for the Social Studies, Washington, D.C., 1971.
A relevant and realistic treatise discussing cultural alternatives and value options using "the voices of youth" as data source. Part III provides instructional guidelines with chapters by Fred Neumann and Donald Oliver on the teacher's role in value issues, Sidney Simon on value clarification strategies, and Donald Oliver and James Shaver on illustrating the use of a unit and teaching materials. Readable pamphlet.

Brown, George Isaac: *Human Teaching for Human Learning: An Introduction to Confluent Education,* The Viking Press, Inc., New York, 1971.
Confluent education is a synthesis of the affective and the cognitive domains or an interplay between them in an effort to make the educational process and the student more human. Describes a pilot program to explore ways to incorporate affective learning activities into the curriculum and to translate some of the activities for use in the classroom. Demonstrates how the classroom experience might deal more effectively with the emotions, feelings, and values of students.

Chazan, Barry I., and Jonas F. Soltis (eds.): *Moral Education,* Teachers College Press, Columbia University, New York, 1973.
"A serious consideration of the nature of morality and the key features of the moral situations viewed from the perspective of the prospective moral educator"— Preface, William Frankena; Philip Phenix, John Wilson, Lawrence Kohlberg, Louis Raths, and others contribute. Part 5 is on teaching and morality.

Childhood Education, vol. 49, no. 5, February 1973, Association for Childhood Education International, Washington, D.C.
See listing in Part II for annotation.

Crittenden, Brian: *Form and Content in Moral Education: An Essay on Aspects of the Mackay Report,* The Ontario Institute for Studies in Education, Toronto, 1972.
The Mackay Report is the Report of the Committee on Religious Education in the Public Schools of the Province of Ontario which took the position that the school should concentrate on the formal features that distinguish moral reasoning and judgment (à la Kohlberg) and not concern itself with the substance of moral beliefs or practices. The author examines critically the adequacy of the Kohlberg theory.

Dennison, George: *The Lives of Children,* Random House, Inc., New York, 1969.
Twenty-three students and three teachers who followed the thought of the "romantics" in education: Neill, Dewey, Holt, Rogers, Kozol, etc. The teachers saw themselves "as an environment for growth and accepted the relationship between the children and themselves as being the very heart of the school."

Educational Leadership, vol. 28, December 1970, Association for Supervision and Curriculum Development, Washington, D.C.

The theme of the issue is "Sensitivity Education: Problems and Promises." Nine articles discuss what sensitivity education is, what research says about it, the need for and importance of it, and practical programs of it in the schools.

Epstein, Charlotte: *Intergroup Relations for the Classroom Teacher,* Houghton Mifflin Company, Boston, 1968.

Suggests that curriculum choices be based on the answer to the question: What is man? Sees interdependence at the core: "How can we perceive in ourselves and in our pupils the small child's capacity for oceanic response, a feeling of oneness with all humankind?" Begins with sixteen anecdotes which illustrate behavioral symptoms of prejudice. Offers a practical and specific guide to teachers for analyzing overt or acknowledged intergroup problems and for helping students recognize and solve them. Replete with suggested materials.

Exploring Human Nature, Education Development Center, Inc., Social Studies Program, Experimental Edition, Cambridge, Mass., 1973.

A year-long upper high school course (three units). Looks at the question of human aggression: Is it inevitable, what are its roots, its cultural manifestations? Asks: How can insights into human behavior be applied to social questions?

Fox, Robert S., Ronald Lippitt, and Eva Schindler-Rainman: *Toward a Humane Society: Images of Potentiality,* Learning Resources Corporation, Fairfax, Va., 1973.

See listing in Part II for annotation.

Goulet, Denis: "An Ethical Model for the Study of Values," *Harvard Educational Review,* vol. 41, May 1971, pp. 205-227.

Suggests that the faculty team must undertake "dialogue until it hurts."

Greenberg, Herbert M.: *Teaching with Feeling: Compassion and Self-Awareness in the Classroom Today,* The Macmillan Company, New York, 1969.

Chapter 1 provides a useful resource for the teacher by listing myths attributed to the teacher, e.g., the myth of callousness, the "I love children" myth, the "I have to know all the answers" myth, and others.

Heath, Douglas H.: "Affective Education: Aesthetics and Discipline," *School Review,* May 1972, pp. 353-370.

1. What are the societal and psychological forces compelling educators to become concerned with the affective growth of students?
2. Can the principal means of affective education be more sharply delineated?
3. Why is affective education a potentially dangerous movement?
4. How can affective education be grounded on a theoretical rationale that integrates it with the academic purposes of the school?

————: *Humanizing Schools: New Directions, New Dimensions,* Hayden Book Company, Inc., New York, 1971.

Describes a model of development in detail and illustrates how it provides a rationale for introducing motivation into the curriculum.

Henderson, James L.: *Education for World Understanding,* Pergamon Press, New York, 1968.

Sketches "a blueprint for an educational system which would encourage the growth of an integrated personality at war neither with itself nor society" by "reviving and reactivating those collective memories of mankind that seem to be the most promising sources of international cooperation today... the subject of this work is the gradual development, in its most expressive manifestations of the consciousness of the universal in man." Specifically, Chapter 2, "Pre-secondary School Possibilities," sketches the outlines of a course of study for children between six and fifteen, and Chapter 5, "The Terrestrial Teacher," expresses the psychology of such a teacher with multinational examples. Chapter 6, "The Promise of Collective Memories," attempts to penetrate more deeply into human motivation, relating it to the types of human behaviors that govern the conduct of world affairs. A unique contribution to developing understandings basic to the mankind view.

Improving Human Relations: Through Classroom, School, and Community Activities, National Council for the Social Studies, Washington, D.C., 1949.
An early work, still useful, reporting classroom activities where inventive teachers have introduced democratic and human values into the lives of their students.

Inlow, Gail M.: *Values in Transition: A Handbook,* John Wiley & Sons, Inc., New York, 1972.
Values to this author are "the determiners in a man that influence his choices in life and that thus decide his behavior." Traditional cultural values, economic values, political values, scientific values, philosophical values, values of the New Left, values of the black community, and a value synthesis receive chapter-length treatment. Outcomes of the developing individual are listed in helpful, first-person fashion (p. 187).

Intergroup Education in Cooperating Schools: *Elementary Curriculum in Intergroup Relations,* American Council on Education, Washington, D.C., 1950.
An early project devoted to improving human relationships in elementary classrooms offers case studies of actual programs undertaken. Describes children's needs as teachers identified them: what needs arose and what steps were taken to provide for them. Chapter 4, "Learning about People"; Chapter 5, "Social Relationships"; and Chapter 6, "Learning to Work and Play Together." Replete with pertinent ideas, though somewhat disjointed in presentation.

Kohlberg, Lawrence: "Stage and Sequence: The Cognitive-Developmental Approach to Socialization," in D. Goslin (ed.), *Handbook of Socialization Theory,* Rand McNally & Company, Chicago, 1969, chap. 6.
A scholarly and thorough presentation of the theory and research upon which the author bases his work, followed by helpful tables and descriptions: "Classification of Moral Judgment into Levels and Stages of Development"; moral stages related to ego types, coded aspects of developing moral judgment, etc.

Kohlberg, Lawrence, and Elliot Turiel: "Moral Development and Moral Education," in G. Lesser (ed.), *Psychology and the Educational Process,* Scott, Foresman and Company, Chicago, 1971, pp. 410-465.
Discuss ethical relativity and culturally universal stages of moral development. Present research findings indicating that much of the failure of communication about values between teachers and children results from discrepancies between

their developmental levels. Suggest ways for the teacher to raise the child's level of thinking and deal with the child's actions.

Leeper, Robert R. (ed.): *Humanizing Education: The Person in the Process,* Association for Supervision and Curriculum Development, Washington, D.C., 1967. Carl Rogers's "The Interpersonal Relationship in the Facilitation of Learning" stresses the attitudinal qualities rather than the intellectual, curricular, or material arrangements for learners. These are described: genuineness in the teachers, prizing, acceptance, trust, and empathic understanding.

Mackey, James A.: "Moral Insight in the Classroom," *The Elementary School Journal,* vol. 73, February 1973, pp. 232—238.
Describes work on a curriculum development project based on a model developed by Lawrence Kohlberg.

Marshall, Bernice (ed.): *Experiences in Being,* Brooks/Cole Publishing Company, Belmont, Calif., 1971.
"The book is an application of humanistic, existential principles to the development of an educational process." In Part I, Floyd Matson speaks of man as man: the concept of man. Articles follow on man with himself and man and his institutions. A dialogue follows most articles, designed to indicate ways of exploring thoughts and feelings. Includes excellent bibliographies for teachers.

Maslow, Abraham H.: *Motivation and Personality,* 2d ed., Harper & Row, Publishers, Incorporated, New York, 1970.
Delineates a hierarchy of human needs: physiological needs, safety needs, needs for love and affection and belonging, needs for personal esteem, and, ultimately, the need for self-actualization. Holds that individuals must satisfy needs at the lower levels before higher needs emerge.

Mayerhoff, Milton: *On Caring,* Harper & Row, Publishers, Incorporated, New York, 1971.
Volume 43 of *World Perspectives,* a series of small books designed to interpret elements of the "creative process which restores man to mankind while deepening and enhancing his communion with the universe." This book successfully accomplishes that purpose. It provides a generalized description of caring as helping "the other" grow through patience, honesty, trust, humility, hope, courage, reciprocation, and constancy.

Moustakas, Clark: *Personal Growth: The Struggle for Identity and Human Values,* Howard A. Doyle Publishing Co., Cambridge, Mass., 1969.
Concentrates on the immediacy of experience as a focus of the learning process. Chapter 3, "The Authentic Self: The Readiness to Be," and Chapter 4, "Authentic and Unauthentic Learning," provide bases for self-understanding by teacher and child. See also his *The Authentic Teacher,* Howard A. Doyle Publishing Co., Cambridge, Mass., 1966.

A Multi-cultural Curriculum for Today's Young Children, Cross-Cultural Family Center, San Francisco, 1969.
A program based on parent planning and participation offers training for helping

parents understand how their feelings about themselves are communicated to their children. Encourages parents to work with the child at home, go on family outings, and work with the child on projects at school.

Patterson, C.H.: *Humanistic Education,* Prentice-Hall, Inc., Englewood Cliffs, N.J., 1973.

Deals with two aspects of humanistic education: teaching subject matter in a more human way and educating the nonintellectual or affective aspects of the student. Rogers, Combs, Maslow, Moustakas, Holt, Dennison, and others provide basic humanistic ideas which the author synthesizes into the framework of teacher and pupil in the classroom setting.

Perceiving, Behaving, Becoming: A New Focus for Education, 1962 Yearbook, Association for Supervision and Curriculum Development, Washington, D.C., 1962.

Earl Kelley's "The Fully Functioning Self," Carl Rogers's "Toward Becoming a Fully Functioning Person," Maslow's "Some Basic Propositions of a Growth and Self-Actualization Psychology," and Arthur Combs's "A Perceptual View of the Adequate Personality" provide tbe base for following sections which extract the most pertinent and promising ideas for teaching.

Peters, Richard S.: "Reason and Habit: The Paradox of Moral Education," in Philip G. Smith (ed.), *Theories of Value and Problems of Education,* The University of Illinois Press, Urbana, 1970, pp. 163-170.

Considers the roles of reason and habit in moral education, suggesting that necessary habits of behavior can be developed in such a way that they do not rule out the development of a rational code.

Piaget, Jean: "The Two Moralities of the Child," in Philip G. Smith (ed.), *Theories of Value and Problems of Education,* The University of Illinois Press, Urbana, 1970, pp. 171-181.

The author reasons that a parallelism exists between moral and intellectual development, and although relations of constraint "contribute to a first type of logical and moral control," relations of cooperation are necessary to bring about the development of intellectual and moral autonomy.

Porter, Nancy, and Nancy Taylor: *How to Assess the Moral Reasoning of Students: A Teachers' Guide to the Use of Lawrence Kohlberg's Stage-Developmental Method,* Hugh Oliver (gen. ed.), The Ontario Institute for Studies in Education, Toronto, 1972.

This guide describes Kohlberg's six stages of moral development and his questionnaires, including nine stories that confront the reader with a moral dilemma. Offers a simplified version of the Kohlberg scoring system so that teachers can assess the moral reasoning of their students. Suggested for use in grade 4 and up.

Richardson, Elizabeth: *The Environment of Learning,* Weybright and Talley, New York, 1967.

A detailed examination by an experienced English educator of the personal relationships within a school community which influence what and how pupils learn.

Rogers, Carl R.: "Interpersonal Relationships: U.S.A. 2000," *Journal of Applied Behavioral Science,* vol. 4, 1968, pp. 265-280.
Sees "continual changingness" as man's greatest problem, advocating a new mode of living openly that stresses the significance of self-awareness and self-actualization. Specific areas of interpersonal relationships within a variety of social institutions are examined. Deals with urban crowding; man-woman relationships; parents and children; persons in industry, religion, and slums.

Rubin, Louis J., and Others: *Facts and Feelings in the Classroom,* Walker and Co., New York, 1973.
See listing in Part II for annotation.

Scheffler, Israel: "Teaching and Telling," in Philip G. Smith (ed.), *Theories of Value and Problems of Education,* The University of Illinois Press, Urbana, 1970, pp. 161-162.
"In moral education we are, in effect, striving to achieve not alone the acquisitions of norms...but the reflective support of norms."

Sherif, Muzafer: *In Common Predicament: Social Psychology of Intergroup Conflict and Cooperation,* Houghton Mifflin Company, Boston, 1966.
The first chapter offers insight into how children develop stereotypes of others. The book discusses the pros and cons of innate aggressiveness. Describes the author's experiments with eleven- and twelve-year-old boys in summer camps, including the Robbers Cave experiment.

Simon, Sidney B., and Others: *Values Clarification: A Handbook of Practical Strategies for Teachers and Students,* Hart Publishing Company, New York, 1972.
Based on Louis Raths' seven processes of valuing, this manual provides seventy-nine specific practical strategies to help build the seven valuing processes into the lives of children. May be used separately or incorporated into standard subject matter at various grade levels.

"Values and Morals: A Volatile Issue in Schools," *Learning,* vol. 1, December 1972, pp. 9-19.
The first article, "Understanding the Hidden Curriculum," describes the moral-education work of Lawrence Kohlberg based on the theory that moral development moves through six sequent stages. The second article, "Doing Something about Values," introduces the values work done by Louis E. Raths and implemented by the values clarification work of Sidney Simon. Following these articles, Simon and Kohlberg compare each other's work.

Zahoric John A., and Dale L. Brubaker: *Toward More Humanistic Instruction,* Wm. C. Brown Company Publishers, Dubuque, Iowa, 1972.
The authors' list of philosophic commitments characteristic of humanistic behavior closely parallels the "commonplaces" of mankind as stated by Goodlad. They present specific behaviors, practices, and strategies that teachers can use in humanizing instruction. Part II, "Humanistic Behavior in the Classroom," deals with teachers' and students' behavior. Part III focuses on ways to begin and further humanistic instruction using gestalt game approaches, case studies, emerging problems, and social action activities. An excellent teacher resource.

PART IV: SUBJECT MATTER IN A MANKIND CURRICULUM

Abrams, Grace C., and Fran C. Schmidt: *Learning Peace: A Resource Unit,* The Jane Addams Peace Association, Philadelphia, 1972.

Intended to help the teacher in grades 7-12 teach about and for peace. Activities for students deal with self-assessment of personal attitudes, examination of conflicts and their resolution, investigation of twentieth-century international peace organizations, and investigation of alternatives to war. Current references to media, literature, and organizations are cited.

Adler Richard R. (ed.): *Humanities Programs Today,* Citation Press, New York, 1970.

Though most of the programs cited are at the secondary level with emphasis on "the" humanities, there is a definite trend in many of the examples toward self-understanding, self-identification, self-expression, man-centered problems, world view, image of man, relationship of self to society, problem solving, and use of inductive methods.

Adventures on a Blue Marble, Southern Association of Colleges and Schools, Atlanta, 1969.

Discusses instructional approaches to international understanding. Gives addresses of all foreign embassies in the U.S. and lists sources for international correspondence.

Agan, Raymond J., and Joseph Hajda (eds.): *Curriculum for Man in an International World,* International Education Year Conference, 1970, Kansas State University, Topeka, 1971.

Contributions by Harold Taylor, Franklin Parker, and Donald Robinson, among others. Arthur J. Lewis, "Continuing Education for World Affairs," charts the relationship between information and attitudes. He proposes "Earth Survival Centers" to promote both. Appendix contains useful bibliographies.

Anthropology Curriculum Project: *Concepts of Culture,* Grades 1 and 4; *The Development of Man and His Culture,* Grades 2 and 5; *Cultural Change,* Grades 3 and 6; University of Georgia, Athens.

A program developed for use in elementary grades.

Anthropology Curriculum Study Project: *History as Cultural Change: An Overview,* The Macmillan Company, New York, 1970.

A sample kit of materials designed to demonstrate how anthropologists study society, outlining some comparative analysis models for use in studying historical data.

————: *Patterns in Human History,* The Macmillan Company, New York, 1971.

Sponsored by the American Anthropological Association, this course offers a teacher's guide plus excellent tools for a social science, cross-disciplinary approach to the study of man.

Approaches to Conflict and Change, Center for War/Peace Studies, David C. King (program director), Thomas Y. Crowell Company, New York, ca. October 1972.

A series of eight, 3 to 4 week units which will help teachers deal with critical issues and concepts involved in significant international concerns.

Arnold, Robert L.: "The Goal: Education for Human Becoming," in Thomas F. Powell (ed.), *Humanities and the Social Studies,* National Council for the Social Studies, Washington, D.C., 1969, pp. 157-172.
   Has implications for the curriculum pertinent to developing a mankind concept. It also suggests some possible qualities for a person with a mankind perspective.

Arnspiger, V. Clyde, Ray W. Rucker, and James A. Brill: *Human Values Series,* K-6, Teacher's Editions, 10 Teaching Pictures, Steck-Vaughn, Austin, Tex., 1967-1970.
   A series of elementary school texts designed to study the shaping and sharing of human values which each person seeks in the social process. Value categories are: respect, power, wealth, enlightenment, skill, well-being, rectitude, and affection. Teaching suggestions and analysis accompany the stories to emphasize each value.

Banks, James A. (ed.): *Teaching Ethnic Studies: Concepts and Strategies,* 43d Yearbook, National Council for the Social Studies, Washington, D.C., 1973.
   Presents conceptual frameworks for studying about ethnic groups; promising strategies and materials; and analyses of institutional racism, social justice, and power relationships in America. Problems of specific ethnic minority groups are treated by members of these groups, providing emotional impact and needed perspective. Excellent bibliographies.

Becker, James: *International Education for Spaceship Earth,* Foreign Policy Association, New York, 1968.
   A short survey of a larger study which summarizes the relationship between man and his environment, needed changes in education and obstacles to change, and strategies for change. See King, David C., and Foreign Policy Association, both listed in this section, referring to the same project directed by James Becker.

Becker, James, and Maurice A. East: *Global Dimensions in U.S. Education: The Secondary School,* Center for War/Peace Studies, New York, 1972.
   Discuss new approaches in the social studies, showing how recent developments apply to international education. Include an analysis of trends, needs, and resources, with recommendations for improving international content and teaching methods.

Becker, James, and Howard D. Mehlinger (eds.): *International Dimensions in the Social Studies,* 1968 Yearbook, National Council for the Social Studies, Washington, D.C., 1968.
   This book proposes that world affairs permeate all social studies, indicating what is being done, the emphasis needed, and useful resources. Discusses area studies, simulation techniques, case method, government programs, and world affairs councils.

Berman, Louise M.: *From Thinking to Behaving: Assignments Reconsidered,* Teachers College Press, Columbia University, New York, 1967.
   Chapter Two, "Activities in the Development of the Thoughtful Person," contains a section on understanding other value systems, defending values, and changing or developing new issues.

———: *New Priorities in the Curriculum,* Charles E. Merrill Books, Inc., Columbus, Ohio, 1968.

Eight human process skills are used as a framework for curriculum rather than traditional school subjects. These are: perceiving, communicating, loving, decision making, knowing, organizing, creating, and valuing. Valuable bibliographies accompany each area of emphasis.

Berman, Louise M. (ed.): *The Humanities and the Curriculum,* Association for Supervision and Curriculum Development, Washington, D.C., 1967.

Louise Berman, "The Humanities: The Present Scene and the Potential"; Earl Johnson, "Some Thoughts on the Relations between the Humanities and the Social Studies"; and Leland Jacobs, "The Potential of the Humanities and the Challenge to Schools," contribute to the study of man.

Blachford, Kevin R.: "What Values?" *Curriculum and Research Bulletin,* vol. 5, August 1970, pp. 100-106.

Discusses three types of values which are vital to education. Behavioral Values imply a mode of conduct in the classroom. Procedural values involve a way of thinking that is important to a given discipline. Substantive values are of two kinds: those necessary to procedural values and those not necessary to procedural values. Substantive values are not to be taught, are nonneutral, need to be freely selected, and should be chosen from among alternatives after thoughtful consideration.

Blumer, Herbert: *Concept of Mankind and Social Studies,* mimeographed paper, Council for the Study of Mankind, Inc., no date.

States the mankind concept has usually been applied to social studies as an ethical recognition of the worth of all people and as knowledge that no division of the human race is superior to other divisions. Suggests a third application: a new interwoven world order with three dimensions: (1) increased *spatial* contact among people; (2) *temporal,* in the form of a rapidly changing world; and (3) *depth,* in the form of greater participation of the common and lower strata of people in the determination of their destinies. To achieve a mankind perspective will require new thinking, concepts, and research from the social sciences.

Borton, Terry: *Reach, Touch, and Teach: Student Concerns and Process Education,* McGraw-Hill Book Company, New York, 1970.

Based on the premise that schooling should provide opportunities for the student to learn processes for coping with his concerns about his inner self and the outside world. The author uses role playing and drama to help students answer the question: Who am I? His "curriculum concerns" include: What is human about human beings? What masks do humans use to hide or express themselves? What happens when people don't hide themselves? How is a personal style developed?

Brearley, Molly (ed.): *The Teaching of Young Children: Some Applications of Piaget's Learning Theory,* Schocken Books Inc., New York, 1969.

Though the book is geared to teachers of the young child, Chapter 8, "Morality: Values and Reasons," will bring insights and understandings to teachers of any age group.

Brown, Ina Corinne: *Understanding Other Cultures,* Prentice-Hall,Inc., Englewood Cliffs, N.J., 1963, paperback.

Helpful book on cultural anthropology to provide the needed frame of reference (cultural patterning) for learning about other peoples.

Building World Sensitivity—Fact or Fiction? An Analysis of International Education as Practiced in Ohio High Schools, Miami University, Department of Educational Administration, Oxford, Ohio, 1972.

A survey which indicates the degree to which international education is being undertaken in Ohio high schools. Sums up with recommendations and guidelines for high school curriculum, staff, and activities.

Carr, William G. (ed.): *Values and the Curriculum: A Report for the Fourth International Curriculum Conference,* 1969, National Education Association of the United States, Center for the Study of Instruction, Washington, D.C., 1970 (Schools for 70's, Auxiliary Series).

Papers examine the relations between social, economic, and political values and programs of education. Wilfred Wees lists aspects of child growth toward a self-directing manhood as (1) self-respect, (2) companionship, (3) independence, and (4) self-appraisal. William O'Neill's helpful discourse on behaving and believing relates values to the process of learning and knowing. Stenhouse adds concreteness in his description of an experiment in humanistic curriculum.

Children and International Education, Association for Childhood Education International, Washington, D.C., 1972.

A portfolio of leaflets designed to acquaint readers with the array of resources available to develop in children and teachers a knowledge and appreciation of others.

Conflict Resolution, Center for Teaching International Relations, University of Denver, Denver.

An experimental curriculum unit providing class assignments, readings, exercises, games, discussion questions, a bibliography, rationale for undertaking the unit, and a set of instructional objectives.

Education for Peace: Focus on Mankind, prepared by the ASCD 1973 Yearbook Committee, George Henderson (chairman and ed.), Association for Supervision and Curriculum Development, Washington, D.C., 1973.

The subject matter of peace education, in this work, includes social justice, social change, ecological balance, and economic welfare, all viewed from a global perspective. It is also concerned with clarification of value perspectives within these fields and an action orientation as well. Viewed from the standpoint of ecology, peace education becomes the study of the mutual interdependence of the systems of man.

Educational Leadership, Journal of the Association for Supervision and Curriculum Development, National Education Association of the United States, Washington, D.C.

See issues of March 1968, vol. 25, "Cross-national or International Education"; and November 1969, vol. 27, "International Cooperation in Education."

Eisner, Elliot W.: *Education and the Idea of Mankind,* mimeographed paper, Council for the Study of Mankind, Inc., no date.

Discusses relationships among the arts, the sciences, and value questions. Gives suggestions on how the introduction of the concept of mankind into the school curriculum might change the subjects and benefit the students. Also suggests the introduction of other fields of social sciences into the curriculum.

Foreign Policy Association: *An Examination of Objectives, Needs and Priorities in International Education in U.S. Secondary and Elementary Schools,* James M. Becker (director) and Lee Anderson (project co-ordinator), Foreign Policy Association—Thomas Y. Crowell Company, New York, 1969.
An extensive study, nationwide, which proposes that curricula develop in students a knowledge and understanding of the world system, a view of the earth as a single planet, man as a single species of life, and his social system as one of many alternatives. Suggests the need for students to examine themselves—their own feelings, sensitivities, and values—and learn not only to work effectively with others but also to assume responsibility for their own actions.

Free and Inexpensive Materials on World Affairs, Teachers College Press, Columbia University, New York, 1969.

Gearing, Frederick O.: "Toward a Mankind Curriculum," *Today's Education,* vol. 59, March 1970, pp. 28-30.
An introduction to two programs using the idea of cultural mapping: *Man: A Course of Study* by Bruner and *Patterns in Human History* by the Anthropology Curriculum Study Project.

Gibson, John S.: *The Intergroup Relations Curriculum: A Program for Elementary School Education,* vol. I, The Lincoln Filene Center for Citizenship and Public Affairs, Tufts University, Medford, Mass., 1969.
Gives background of the Center's research and development on IRC and the propositions, critiques, and recommendations with respect to intergroup relations education in the U.S. Reports on the Center's in-service programs for teachers, evaluation instruments, and procedures for disseminating information and findings regarding the curriculum. Volume II of this study presents the curriculum and is issued separately. It includes the conceptual framework of the "governing process," methodological tools, recommendations for teaching, learning activities and units, and recommended instructional resources for teachers and students.

Global Development Studies: Model Curriculum for Secondary Schools and Under-graduate Colleges, Management Institute for National Development, 230 Park Avenue, New York 10017, 1973.
A year-long course in the global nature of today's social, political, and business affairs designed to offer a world perspective that helps students "see themselves and their society as an inseparable part of the global community of societies." Aims to develop conscious attitudes toward one's own belief and conceptions and toward the beliefs and conceptions of others. Organizations and relevant periodical literature are listed as well as pertinent bibliographies with sources.

Global Dimensions in U.S. Education, Center for War/Peace Studies, New York, 1972.
Four studies published jointly by the Education Commission of the International Studies Association, the Committee on Pre-Collegiate Education of the American

Political Science Association, and the Center for War/Peace Studies: *The Elementary School,* by Judith V. Torney and Donald N. Morris (see listing in this section under Torney for annotation): *The Secondary School,* by James M. Becker and Maurice A. East (see listing in this section under Becker for annotation); *The University,* by Maurice Harari; and *The Community,* by William C. Rogers.

Goldberg, Maxwell H.: *The Humanities and Mankind Teaching,* mimeographed paper, Council for the Study of Mankind, Inc., no date.
Relates the mutual benefits of introducing the concept of mankind to the new drive and emphasis on the humanities. Emphasizes emotional commitment as well as rational understanding of the concept of mankind in the humanities. Cites the need for values in education. Identifies three conceptions of mankind: (1) the sum total of all humans, past, present, and future; (2) mankind as fact by faith; and (3) the name for ideal man. States that the latter two conceptions have more functional meaning for those attempting to teach in mankind perspective.

————: "Humanities Teaching and the Mankind Emphasis," *School and Society,* vol. 99, 1971, pp. 176-178.
Discusses ways in which the mankind concept could strengthen humanities courses. The major way identified is in the unifying, interdisciplinary quality of the concept of mankind. Calls for the development of a stockpile of templates and packages of selected materials for any type of humanities offerings.

Goldschmidt, Walter: *Exploring the Ways of Mankind,* Holt, Rinehart and Winston, Inc., New York, 1960.
A cultural anthropology reference to provide the necessary background for understanding the commonalities of peoples from diverse cultures. Easy to read.

Goodlad, John I.: "The Objectives of American Education and the Interdependent World," *Indiana Social Studies Quarterly,* vol. XVIII, Winter 1965-1966, pp. 8-16.
The concept of mankind is presented as a necessary base upon which education must be built if we are to deal with the increasing interdependence in the world today. Offers guidelines to program development.

————: *Some Propositions in Search of Schools,* National Education Association of the United States, Washington, D.C., 1962.
Identifies the desired product of the educative process as the development of rational men. Suggests four significant aspects of schooling—facilities, expectations, curriculum, and method—as means toward attaining the goal.

Goodman, Mary Ellen: *The Culture of Childhood: Child's-Eye Views of Society and Culture,* Teachers College Press, Columbia University, New York, 1970.
The manner in which children in different societies see themselves and are seen by adults; the values and attitudes that children take from others or discover for themselves: from the Philippines, Java, Puerto Rico, New Zealand (the Maori), Japan, Mexico, China, and Egypt, and in the United States includes the Amish, the Negroes, and other Americans. Discusses training of children, patterns of politeness, occupational preferences, play, language habits, peer cultures, etc. Chapter 6, "Values and Conscience," is especially pertinent.

Grambs, Jean Dresden: *Intergroup Education: Methods and Materials,* sponsored by the Anti-Defamation League of B'nai B'rith, Prentice-Hall, Inc., Englewood Cliffs, N.J., 1968.

Offers specific suggestions for the classroom teacher: sources and ways of using them. Part I is a brief look at who needs intergroup education; Part II describes promising practices including examples of open-ended materials and role playing; Part III, the major portion of the book, is a fully annotated bibliography arranged by useful topics, including organizations, journals, and other bibliographies. A practical guide.

Griffin, Willis H., and Ralph B. Spence: *Cooperative International Education,* Association for Supervision and Curriculum Development, Washington, D.C., 1970. The Great Education proposed here "must deal with attitudes." Some of the basic assumptions held: "New insights into human behavior; increasingly refined concepts of social change; and invention of new means of communicating, teaching and learning make possible" a vastly superior education; "development is a social process...it relates to matters of human spirit and will, values and aspirations, human relationships."

Harvard Social Studies Project, see *Public Issues Series/Harvard Social Studies Project* in this section.

Hunkins, Ralph H.: *Education for International Understanding: A Critical Appraisal of the Literature,* unpublished Ed.D. dissertation, Indiana University, School of Education, Bloomington, 1968.

Categorizes the positions of leading writers, attempting to pinpoint the definitions they use in order to clarify their various stances and their views: "IU-K" is used for international understanding—knowledge of people; "IU-IN" is used for international understanding—intentions of others; and "IU-A" is used for international understanding—attitudes.

Hunt, Maurice P., and Lawrence E. Metcalf: *Teaching High School Social Studies,* 2d ed., Harper & Row, Publishers, Incorporated, 1968.

See the teacher's task as that of helping each student improve his own capacity for perception. Define learning as an expansion of insight, a moving to higher levels; effective learning taking place in situations where beliefs and attitudes are challenged, where something is at stake. Provide a sound rationale for the reflective method of teaching.

Ianni, Francis A. S.: *Culture, System, and Behavior: The Behavioral Sciences and Education,* Science Research Associates, Inc., Chicago, 1967.

The author illustrates in clear and concise style the contributions that the disciplines of anthropology, sociology, and psychology, in particular, can make to the understanding of man and the study of education. In anthropology, he treats the concepts of culture, socialization, values, acculturation, and social organization. In sociology, he relates the concepts of groups, stratification and society stature and role, social interaction, and social systems to education and the schools.

Indiana Social Studies Quarterly, vol. XVII, Autumn 1964, Ball State University, Muncie, Ind.

The theme of the volume is "World History: The Mankind Perspective." A series of four articles directed at the teaching of history at the secondary level. Authors discuss concepts and approaches they consider important in making world history more in keeping with a mankind history.

————, vol. XVIII, Winter 1965-1966, Ball State University, Muncie, Ind.
Contains four articles presented at a conference on elementary school social studies sponsored by the Johnson Foundation and under the auspices of the Council for the Study of Mankind, Inc. The articles suggest new approaches, new processes, and new uses for the social studies and some of the social sciences. The suggestions have implications for subject matter in a mankind curriculum.

Intercom, vol. 13, no. 2, March-April 1971, "Teaching about War, Peace, Conflict, and Change," Center for War/Peace Studies, New York.
A useful brief résumé of ongoing efforts, including a discussion of affective development, the concept approach, values, and subject matter. The appendix explores in detail the work of the Center for Teaching International Relations, Graduate School of International Studies, University of Denver; the Harvard Social Studies Project, School of Education, Harvard University; and the World Law Fund. Also includes annotated listing of additional publications or organizations.

International Peace Research Newsletter, vol. 11, nos. 1 and 2, Spring 1973, "Special Issue on Peace Education," Christoph Wulf (guest ed.), International Peace Research Association, Oslo 3, Norway (P.O. Box 5052).
This issue includes topics: "Making the School an Instrument for Peace" (Geneva, Switzerland); "Institute for World Order" (New York); "Teaching—Models for Social Science" (Frankfurt, Germany); "Developing a Curriculum for Peace Education" (Netherlands); etc.

Johnson, Earl S.: "Some Thoughts on the Relations between the Humanities and the Social Studies," in *The Humanities and the Curriculum,* Association for Supervision and Curriculum Development, Washington, D.C., 1967, pp. 9-21.
Provides a rationale for a mankind curriculum: "Without an adequate grasp of man's experience as *Mankind's* experience, this generation will be ill-taught about the civilization to which it has become heir. . . ." Sees the principles of continuity and universality in human affairs as the essence of humanism. Develops a "way of mankind."

Jones, Richard M.: *Fantasy and Feeling in Education,* University Press, New York, 1968.
Discusses the relationship of the humanistic education emphasis on feeling to Bruner's *Man: A Course of Study,* an unfeeling curricular innovation, in Jones's eyes. Shows how that effort could have been improved, offering specific creative ideas for so doing. Uses Erikson's chart of development.

Keating, Charlotte M.: *Building Bridges of Understanding between Cultures,* Palo Verde Pub. Co., Tucson, Ariz., 1971.
A bibliography of children's literature fully annotated and grouped under topic by three levels of schooling, selected to develop an understanding and appreciation of the world's cultural diversity.

Kelley, Earl C., and Marie J. Rasey: *Education and the Nature of Man,* Harper & Brothers, New York, 1952.

The nature of the human organism is clearly and briefly described and then applied in areas of learning and of human relations. Part II states some practices in teaching which are indicated by modern research. The teacher's task is seen as one of facilitating growth through better communications, cooperation, freedom, creativity, and evaluation. The chapter on method suggests involvement, participation, and communication, enhanced by small-group work, teacher-pupil planning, and everything that brings teacher and pupil together in the learning process. Chapter 14, "The Next Development of Man," emphasizes the unitary principle in all life and all things: "Man and his environment are one....We will modify our attitudes toward boundaries and barriers [national boundaries too]. The common people are more ready to hold to peaceful attitude toward all peoples than is usually realized....Mankind could be made over by our educational institutions if learning proper relationship became as important as learning to multiply or spell." Children learn from the *way* we act.

Kenworthy, Leonard S.: *The International Dimension of Education,* National Education Association of the United States, Association for Supervision and Curriculum Development, Washington, D.C., 1971.
Examines aspects of change in the world, the need for "internationally-minded individuals," and implications for teaching including strategies and materials. Bibliographies are useful.

King, David C.: *International Education for Spaceship Earth,* Foreign Policy Association—Thomas Y. Crowell Company, New York, 1970 (New Dimensions, no. 4).
Based on the Foreign Policy Association study cited earlier in this section. Part I is a digest of the full report: educational needs for "spaceship earth," where all inhabitants have a common destiny and earth is a single interlocked world system; obstacles to change. Part II offers strategies for change, experimental curriculum projects, and innovative teaching methods. Useful readings and bibliographies throughout. Useful chapter on simulation games.

King, Edith W.: *Worldmindedness: The World—Context for Teaching in the Elementary School,* Wm. C. Brown Company Publishers, Dubuque, Iowa, 1971.
"A teacher's text describing and outlining the teaching of worldmindedness through the school curriculum and particular emphasis on the arts and social studies as channels." Bibliography and appendixes provide excellent resource suggestions.

————: *The Young Child and Social Education for a World Society,* paper prepared for the Social Science Education Consortium Roundup, Denver, June 1972.
Develops the notion of putting world-mindedness into the early childhood curriculum. Cites projects both in England and in the U.S. that provide learning experiences for children in social awareness and multicultural perspectives.

Kohlberg, Lawrence: "Moral Education in the Schools: A Developmental View," *The School Review,* vol. 74, Spring 1966, pp. 1-30.
Reports research findings on the development of moral character relevant to moral education in the schools which suggest slowly developing formation of cognitive principles of moral judgment and decision and of related ego abilities. Research

also suggests that it may be possible for the teacher to stimulate the development of moral character in the school by creating a classroom atmosphere encouraging participation, communicating his own values with regard to broader and more genuinely moral issues than classroom rules, having the child become involved in genuine and difficult moral conflicts, and getting the child to examine the pros and cons of his conduct in his own terms.

Krathwohl, David R., B. S. Bloom, and B. B. Masia: *Taxonomy of Educational Objectives: Handbook II, The Affective Domain,* David McKay, Inc., New York, 1964.

A guide to setting objectives with concern for valuing, commitment, conceptualization of a value, organization of a value system, etc.

Krug, Mark M.: *Introduction: History and the Idea of Mankind,* mimeographed paper, Council for the Study of Mankind, Inc., no date.

Cites examples of how world history has been largely of a Western perspective. Also cites the need for a mankind history. Discusses several attempts to develop a more universal world history. Ends with a proposal for a book to be published under the auspices of the Council for the Study of Mankind, Inc. The purpose of the book is to examine the extent to which the existence and common destiny of mankind were present in the ages of past history.

Learning to Live as Neighbors, Association for Childhood Education International, Washington, D.C., 1972.

A carefully chosen collection of articles reprinted from *Childhood Education,* arranged under three classifications: general philosophy, methodology, and case studies. The articles were selected to review ideas related to a new three-year project, Neighbors Unlimited, focusing on international and intercultural relations in school, home, and community. Also see *Suggestions for Implementing Project: Neighbors Unlimited,* Association for Childhood Education International, Washington, D.C., 1972.

Lippitt, Ronald, Robert Fox, and Lucille Schaible: *Social Science Resource Book,* Science Research Associates, Inc., Chicago, 1969.

Readings for students to advance their use of social science on: behavior specimen, observation, cause and effect, multiple causation, circular process, asking questions. Unit 2, "Discovering Differences"; Unit 3, "Friendly and Unfriendly Behavior"; Unit 4, "Being and Becoming"; Unit 5, "Individuals and Groups"; Unit 6, "Deciding and Doing"; Unit 7, "Influencing Each Other."

Low, Robert G., and Lawrence E. Metcalf (eds.): *The Individual and World Order: Human Rights and Responsibilities,* World Law Fund, New York, 1971.

Selected readings which highlight the problems of individual rights and responsibilities, especially in war situations.

Macdonald, James B., Bernice J. Wolfson, and Esther Zaret: *Reschooling Society: A Conceptual Model,* Association for Supervision and Curriculum Development, Washington, D.C., 1973.

See listing in Part II for annotation.

Magnelia, Paul F.: "The Inter-Nation Simulation and Secondary Education," *Journal of Creative Behavior,* vol. 3, Spring 1969, pp. 115-121.

The author found that this topic of simulation exercise was effective on a secondary school level. He found it to have the capacity to reach out and involve students of supposed low ability.

Man: A Course of Study, Education Development Center, Inc., Cambridge, Mass., 1969.

A one-year course for upper elementary grades instigated by Jerome S. Bruner and developed by the Social Studies Curriculum Program of EDC. Student materials taken from ethnographic film studies and field research are used to explore the roots of man's social behavior through the study of selected animal groups and a remote human society.

Metcalf, Lawrence E. (ed.): *Values Education: Rationale, Strategies, and Procedures,* 41st Yearbook, National Council for the Social Studies, Washington, D.C., 1971.

The first chapter attempts to answer the question: What exactly are the legitimate objectives of value analysis in the classroom? The answers given: helping students develop the capabilities to do so, and teaching students how to resolve value conflict between themselves and others. Chapter 2 gives teaching strategies for the above objectives.

Miel, Alice, and Louise Berman (eds.): *In the Minds of Men: Educating the Young People of the World,* Association for Supervision and Curriculum Development, Washington, D.C., 1970.

Report of the World Conference on Education sponsored by the ASCD Commission on International Cooperation in Education. Participants from various countries.

Mind Your World: A Citizen's Guide to International Understanding, U.S. National Commission for UNESCO, Washington, D.C., 1969.

Mitchell, Morris R.: *World Education: Revolutionary Concept,* Pageant Press, Inc., New York, 1967.

Describes the development of a program of higher education with central emphasis on man's major problems, using the world as a campus, and describes the search for a unified perspective on man. Involvement is a key word in attempts to deepen human affection, to attune one to the social and cosmic forces, and to strengthen personal convictions leading to action. Chapter IV, "A Rash of World Education Places," describes other such programs.

Moyer, Joan E.: *Bases for World Understanding and Cooperation: Suggestions for Teaching the Young Child,* National Education Association of the United States, Association for Supervision and Curriculum Development, Washington, D.C., 1970.

Focus is on process skills (see Berman), with selected generalizations to serve as guidelines for teachers. Suggestions for varied opportunities for experiences (action proposals) contributing to the understanding of the generalizations are offered. The author stresses the need for parents and teachers to work together and the need for a world-minded teacher.

Multicultural Social Education Program—First Year: People Are Both Alike and Different, Southwest Educational Development Laboratory, Austin, Tex. 1969.

An experimental unit designed to provide an opportunity "to develop rational understanding of cultural diversity." Activities attempt to illustrate the common humanity of people.

Nesbitt, William A. (ed): *Data on the Human Crisis: A Handbook for Inquiry,* Center for International Programs, New York State Education Department, New York, 1972.
Data and graphs on aspects of war and peace—past, present, and future. Teacher's guide includes suggestions for data inquiry experiences and information. Just what teachers need.

————: *Teaching about War and Its Control: A Selective Annotated Bibliography for the Social Studies Teacher,* State Education Department, Albany, N.Y., 1972.
Designed to aid the teacher in considering both what to teach about war and peace and how best to teach it. Topics include nationalism, U.S. foreign policy, modern war, and ethics and morality. Calls attention to the value of using films, simulations, and case studies as well as using data and scenarios. Excellent teacher resource.

Newman, Arthur: *Select Bibliography: International Education,* mimeographed paper, University of Florida, Gainesville, 1971.
A useful and current listing developed for the author's course in International Education at the University of Florida. Some headings used: "Universal Man," "World Community," "Perception," and "Communication."

Northeastern States Youth Citizenship Project: *Ideology and World Affairs: A Resource Unit for Teachers,* Tufts University, The Lincoln Filene Center for Citizenship and Public Affairs, Medford, Mass., 1963.
Developed at the Workshop for Teachers on Basic Issues in Citizenship, held at Tufts University in July 1962. John S. Gibson provided content held to enhance the background of classroom teachers involved. Instructional resources are fully annotated and keyed to the appropriate learning experiences developed in the text.

Nye, Vernice T., Robert E. Nye, and H. Virginia Nye: *Toward World Understanding with Song,* Wadsworth Publishing Company, Inc., Belmont, Calif.
This fine collection of songs helps view other people and their culture through their music.

Ojemann, Ralph H.: *Developing a Program for Education in Human Behavior,* Educational Research Council of Greater Cleveland, Cleveland, Ohio, 1967.
Based on the need for the teacher to demonstrate in his daily behavior an understanding approach toward each student. Contributes to the student's understanding of his social environment; uses demonstrations furnished by the teacher's behavior, narratives for children, and casually oriented social problems, and uses a room council as a laboratory for applying the understanding of behavior dynamics to "real" situations.

Oswald, James M.: *Earthship—Fluid Geography of Three-dimensional Spaceship Earth,* Manual for Teachers, Phase I, part A, World Law Fund, New York, 1972.
A brief outline of objectives and classroom activities to develop "earthmanship,"

the improvement of understanding, communications, and relationship among peoples on "spaceship earth." Exploratory material based on geographic concepts.

Pelto, Pertti J.: *The Study of Anthropology,* George D. Spindler (consultant), Charles E. Merrill Books, Inc., Columbus, Ohio, 1965.
The section "Suggested Methods for Teachers" gives the teacher-anthropologist helpful ideas to initiate classroom activities. Also includes suggested readings and classroom materials.

Phenix, Philip H.: *Man and His Becoming,* Rutgers University Press, New Brunswick, N.J., 1964.
I. "Being and Becoming Human": the contribution of mathematics and the natural sciences; uses "body," "mind," and "spirit" as useful terms in discovering a person's nature and activity, but insists on the unity of man. For instance, in mathematics, the thinker can exhibit the basis for thought, thought becoming conscious of itself, leading to self-awareness. II. "Being and Becoming Related": What is known of man from the social sciences. III. "Being and Becoming Oneself": What is known of man from the humanities.

Phi Delta Kappa Teacher Education Project on Human Rights: *A Guide for Improving Teacher Education in Human Rights,* University of Oklahoma, Norman, 1971.
Designed to improve pre-service and in-service programs in the area of basic human rights and values. Gertrude Noar did most of the writing. Includes foundations for a human rights program in education, exploration, institutional and teacher behavior in human rights, practical approaches to the teaching of human rights, and an extensive bibliography.

Phi Delta Kappan, vol. 50, no. 8, 1969.
Contains articles on the teaching of values by Joseph Junell, essentialist, "Can Our Schools Teach Moral Commitment?"; Maurice P. Hunt, relativist, "Some Views on Situational Morality"; and Jack R. Fraenkel, "Value Education in the Social Studies."

Piaget, Jean: *The Moral Judgment of the Child,* The Free Press, New York, 1965.
Shows that children build up a sense of duty in their relations to the world around them. Early sense of right and wrong comes from responding to rules of adults. An "external conventionality" is developed—a stage each child must go through before advancing to a higher stage. He must be guided from the stage at which values are externally imposed to that at which he makes more and more of his own value decisions.

Preston, Ralph C. (ed.): *Teaching World Understanding,* Prentice-Hall, Inc., New York, 1955.
An early collection of ideas for developing understanding of the people of the world among young people. Based on the Quaker objective: the development of a deep respect for human personality wherever and however it may be found.

Project Survival: International Education for the Seventies in Glens Falls, Glens Falls City Schools, Glens Falls, N.Y., 1970.
Includes a "Working Paper" and "Teachers' Survival Kit." Primary goal is to develop an increased understanding of the world as a global system and mankind

as a single human community. The antecedent program is described in Bulletin 35 of the National Council for the Social Studies, *Improving the Teaching of World Affairs: The Glens Falls Story,* and Curriculum Series 13, *Bringing the World into Your Classroom.*

Public Issues Series/Harvard Social Studies Project, Grades 9-12, American Educational Publications, Columbus, Ohio, 1971.
A series of paperbacks adopted from the Harvard project conducted by Donald W. Oliver and Fred M. Newmann which employ controversial case studies to motivate students in vital public issues and help them analyze and discuss persisting human dilemmas. Oliver and Newmann authored the accompanying teaching guide, *Cases and Controversy,* emphasizing conflict of values and emergent values. Forces the student to look at his personal value system.

Raths, Louis E.: *Values and Teaching: Working with Values in the Classroom,* Charles E. Merrill Books, Inc., Columbus, Ohio, 1966.
Presents a comprehensive methodology for the clarification of values in a classroom setting. Indoctrination of the student with specific values is not the goal. Rather, the student is helped to clarify what his values are, and to examine the consequences of these values for him. The book is clearly written and almost any teacher should be able to utilize it for integrating value clarification into everyday classroom activities.

Raths, Louis E., et al.: *Teaching for Thinking: Theory and Application,* Charles E. Merrill Books, Inc., Columbus, Ohio, 1967.
Thinking in this book is not restricted to the cognitive domain; it includes expression of values, attitudes, feelings, beliefs, and aspirations. It is conceived as processes associated with inquiry, problem solving, and decision making. Behavior patterns are described which characterize poor thinking skills, with examples given of techniques used to foster more creative thinking.

Read, Herbert: *Education for Peace,* Charles Scribner's Sons, New York, 1949.
"Mankind must be predisposed for peace by the right kind of education:...all who are engaged in the actual shaping or manipulation of materials, in what we call creative activities, lack any evident desire to give expression to their destructive impulses.... The moral regeneration of mankind can be accomplished by moral education, and until moral education is given priority over all other forms of education, I see no hope for the world. I have already indicated what I mean by moral education—*not* education by moral precept, but education by moral practice, which in effect means education by aesthetic discipline, and in the chapters that follow, I shall try to describe in more detail the principles and methods of this kind of education."

The Record, vol. 70, no. 6, March 1969, "Hand in Hand for World Understanding," special issue, Teachers College, Columbia University, New York.

Report of the Conference on History and Mankind, mimeographed paper, Council for the Study of Mankind, Inc., no date.
Summaries of presentations at the conference concerned primarily with the possibility of, problems in, and need for a mankind history. Issues in defining the concept

of mankind and a history of mankind are identified but not resolved. One of the most productive and recurring ideas was of the universalities that bind men together and how these, if they exist, may be identified and fostered.

Rose, Caroline B.: *Sociology,* Charles E. Merrill Books, Inc., Columbus, Ohio, 1965. A handbook of sociology which outlines what sociologists study, their methodology, basic understandings, important research studies, and developments. The final chapter cites four generalizations drawn from the previous content of the book and gives suggestions on how the generalizations might be developed at various educational levels, including the elementary school levels.

Rose, Peter: *The Subject Is Race,* Oxford University Press, New York, 1968. Reviews the history of thoughts and ideas on race by early social scientists. Describes actual classroom practice in teaching race relations courses, suggesting ways to improve teaching in the light of advanced findings in this field.

Sady, Rachel Reese: *Anthropology and the Idea of Mankind,* mimeographed paper, Council for the Study of Mankind, Inc., no date. Proposes three themes from anthropology relevant to the concept of mankind: (1) biological basis for unity of man, (2) existence of cultural diversity within a common human pattern, and (3) universality of processes of culture change. Discusses the importance of examining cultures for universal patterns as well as diversities. Diversities must always be considered in relation to *development and function.* Discusses ways in which cultures change.

Scriven, Michael: *Morality,* Publication 122 of the Social Science Education Consortium, U.S. Office of Education Cooperative Research Program, Purdue University, Lafayette, Ind., 1966.

————: *Student Values as Educational Objectives,* Publication 124.

————: *Value Claims in the Social Sciences,* Publication 123. *Morality* is a position paper on the foundations of ethics and the methodological basis for moral value judgments. *Value Claims in the Social Sciences* brings that position to bear on value issues in the social sciences. *Student Values as Educational Objectives* deals with the role of values in the curriculum.

Shaftel, Fannie R., and George Shaftel: *Role Playing for Social Values: Decision-Making in the Social Studies,* Prentice-Hall, Inc., Englewood Cliffs, N.J., 1967. Develops both theory and practice to guide users, including a checklist for guiding role playing. The second part provides "problem stories" for developing individual integrity, group responsibility, and self-acceptance.

Shane, Harold G.: "International Education in the Elementary and Secondary School," *The United States and International Education,* 68th Yearbook, part I, National Society for the Study of Education, The University of Chicago Press, Chicago, 1969, pp. 269-297. Using Hall and Traeger's "universals" (see Hall entry, Part I), Shane develops a "culture ring model" as a basis for curriculum development and related teaching practices. The idea is to map the terrain of culture by utilizing Hall's primary message system on basic human activities.

Shane, Harold G. (ed.): *The United States and International Education,* 68th Yearbook, part I, National Society for the Study of Education, The University of Chicago Press, Chicago, 1969.
Chapter III by Arnold Anderson, "Challenges and Pitfalls in International Education," and Chapter XI by Harold Shane, "International Education in the Elementary and Secondary School," are especially noteworthy.

Sizer, Nancy F., and Theodore R. Sizer (eds.): *Moral Education: Five Lectures,* Harvard University Press, Cambridge, Mass., 1970.
Contains: James M. Gustafson, "Education for Moral Responsibility"; Richard S. Peters, "Concrete Principles and the Rational Passion"; Lawrence Kohlberg, "Education for Justice"; Bruno Bettelheim, "Moral Education"; and Kenneth Keniston, "Youth and Violence: The Contexts of Moral Crisis."

Social Education, vol. 31, no. 1, January 1967, section: "The Elementary School: Focus on Values," pp. 34-48.
Includes Melvin Eger's "Value Teaching in the Middle and Upper Grades: Rationale for Teaching but Not Transmitting Values."

————, vol. 32, no. 7, November 1968, "International Education for the Twenty-first Century."
An expanded issue devoted to the international dimension of the social studies curriculum with a view to what schools should offer students. Much of the writing is based on the Foreign Policy Association study *An Examination of Objectives, Needs and Priorities* cited earlier in this section.

————, vol. 34, no. 1, January 1970, "International Relations: Ideas and Issues."
Discusses the question: "Are national self-interest and world peace compatible?" Also, communication analysis, the world population crisis, influence of disarmament and realism, and a space age curriculum are discussed.

Sociological Resources for the Social Studies, Ann Arbor, Mich.: *Episodes in Social Inquiry Series,* Allyn and Bacon, Inc., Boston, 1969-1971.
Teachers are urged to help their students directly confront feelings of prejudice and the unconscious acceptance of discrimination. Episodes on stereotypes ("Images of People"), on race relations ("Class and Race in the United States"), and on poverty ("The Incidence and Effects of Poverty in the U.S.") offer opportunities for students to encounter relevant evidence and analyze it.

Some Suggestions on Teaching and Human Rights, UNESCO, Paris, 1968.
A brief summing up of practical experience by teachers and schools in various countries as they attempted to promote better understanding of the principles of human rights. The appendix includes the Universal Declaration of Human Rights.

Star Power, Simile II, P.O. Box 1023, La Jolla, Calif. 92037.
A simulation role-playing game creates a situation in which the student develops an empathic understanding of the results of unequal distribution of resources.

Stavrianos, Leften: *A Global History of Man,* Allyn and Bacon, Inc., Boston, 1966.
This text provides students with information about human similarities in order for them to compare various world societies.

Strauss, Jack, and Richard Dufour: "Discovering Who I Am: Humanities Course

for Sixth Grade Students," *Elementary English,* vol. 47, January 1970, pp. 85-120.
A six-week unit designed to probe into the problem of identity· and to share
with students the ways, the means, and the values of investigating the measuring
of human experience, in this case their own experiencing. Concentrates on role
playing to explore group behavior and the dilemmas of the child as he searches
for his identity and his personal values.

Summerfield, Geoffrey (ed.): *Man: For High Schools,* Grades 9-12, McDougal, Littell
& Co., Evanston, Ill., 1971.
A high school literature series designed to develop an awareness of what it feels
like to be alive in the twentieth century, a sense of life's possibilities, and the
idea of the universality of man. Outstanding contemporary authors are included.

Theory into Practice, vol. X, no. 3, June 1971, "A Regeneration of the Humanities."
Includes Lawrence Stenhouse's description of the Humanities Curriculum Project
in England and Barry MacDonald's holistic approach to its evaluation. Peter
Dow, in his report on *Man: A Course of Study,* cites Paulo Freire and Richard
Jones and the way their ideas might enhance the use of that course. Jerry Walker
suggests that all humanities programs should become continuing seminars where
all students come together to explore their common humanity.

Thompson, Laura: *The Secret of Culture,* Random House, Inc., New York, 1969.
Like Brown, Thompson provides basic understandings in the field of cultural
anthropology.

Tolley, Howard, Jr.: *Children and War: Political Socialization to International
Conflict,* Teachers College Press, Columbia University, New York, 1973.
Reports a survey of 2,677 children aged seven to fifteen, examining how and
when children acquire attitudes toward war (specifically the Vietnam War) and
what the primary sources of children's information are.

Torney, Judith V., and Donald N. Morris: *Global Dimensions in U.S. Education:
The Elementary School,* Center for War/Peace Studies, New York, 1972.
Review important studies of international attitudes and attitude formation in children. Describe several current programs in the U.S. attempting to improve international content in elementary school curriculum. See the period of middle childhood
as especially important in the formation of attitudes.

Utah State Board of Education: *Focus on Man, a Prospectus: Social Studies for
Utah Schools,* Utah State Board of Education, Salt Lake City, 1972.
Takes the traditional "expanding communities" approach, but the guiding questions
asked about selected focal points at various levels may offer suggestions for pertinent
activities especially in areas of: recognition of the dignity and worth of the individual,
the use of intelligence to improve human living, and the effective development
of moral and ethical values.

Ward, Barbara: *The Lopsided World,* W. W. Norton & Company, New York,
1968.
Writer-economist Ward contrasts the people of the rich and poor nations as she
does in *Spaceship Earth* (Columbia University Press, New York, 1966) and *Five
Ideas That Changed the World* (W. W. Norton and Company, New York, 1959).

Wax, Murray L., Stanley Diamond, and Fred Gearing (eds.): *Anthropological Perspectives on Education,* Basic Books, Inc., Publishers, New York, 1971.
A set of original essays together with an international bibliography.

Weinstein, Gerald, and Mario D. Fantini (eds.): *Toward Humanistic Education: A Curriculum of Affect,* a Ford Foundation Report, Frederick A. Praeger, Inc., New York, 1970.
The report examines the role of affective behavior in determining the substance and process of elementary schooling. Chapter II analyzes the nature of instructional relevance, the behavioristic goals of education, and the relation between cognition and affect. Chapter III presents the model developed to help teachers in developing, evaluating, and using a curriculum based on children's concerns. Chapters IV through VIII illustrate lessons, units, and techniques used in classrooms.

Wells, Harold C., and John T. Canfield: *About Me,* Student Book and Teacher's Guide, Combined Motivation Education Systems, Inc., Rosemont, Ill., 1971.
Distributed by Encyclopaedia Britannica Educational Corporation, Chicago.
A workshop for mankind teachers, held at UCLA during the summer of 1972, found this material helpful in developing self-concepts of upper elementary school children. The work was based on the belief that more fully functioning human beings will have a deep commitment to mankind.

Wilson, John, et al.: *Introduction to Moral Education,* Penguin Books, Inc., Baltimore, 1967.
One of the few books available which offer substantial assistance to teachers in developing understanding in this field of endeavor.

The World without War Game, World without War Publications, 7245 South Merrill Avenue, Chicago, Ill. 60649.
Students experience group conflict dynamics that present them with realistic alternatives to war.

Wulf, Christoph (ed.): *Handbook on Peace Education,* International Peace Research Association, Education Committee, Frankfurt/Main-Oslo, 1974.
Includes contributions from all parts of the world involving the issues of conflict theory, development theory, and international structures. Elise Boulding's "The Child and Non-violent Social Change" develops a socialization model drawing from several different disciplinary frameworks. Part III, "Reports on Approaches to Peace Education in Different Countries," shows what is actually in progress.

PART V:
PERTINENT PERIODICALS

Atlas, 1180 Avenue of the Americas, New York, N.Y. 10036.

Childhood Education, Journal of the Association for Childhood Education International, Washington, D.C. 20016.

Frequently deals with pertinent issues, especially the numbers: March 1965, "The World and the Classroom"; October 1965, "Building on Cultural Differences"; January 1969, "Beyond Ourselves—Toward Deeper Understanding"; and May 1971, "The World House: Building a Qualitative Environment for All the World's Children."

Current, Plainfield, Vt. 05667.

The Cooperator, joint publication of the International Cooperating Council and the Cooperators, Northridge, Calif.
ICC long-range objective: To foster the emergence of a new universal man and civilization based upon unity in diversity among all peoples. Cooperating organizations consist of religious and secular groups. The Cooperators are initiating a major effort to form a universal religion.

Fields within Fields...within Fields: The Methodology of the Creative Process, World Institute Council, New York City, Julius Stulman (publisher).
"Climbing to Mankind Solutions," vol. 1, no. 3, 1968, "Man's Emergent Evolution," vol. 3, no. 1, 1970, contains articles by Willis H. Harman, "Alternate Futures and Habitability," and A. H. Maslow, "Towards a Humanistic Biology."

Intercom, Center for War/Peace Studies, 218 East 18th Street, New York, N.Y. 10003.
A guide to the world affairs field.

International Understanding at School, UNESCO Associated Schools Project, published twice a year.
This bulletin for Associated Schools contains articles on subjects of interest to participating schools, news on projects, requests for collaboration or assistance, notes on publications and documents, etc. A useful resource for information concerning ongoing programs.

Manas, Manas Publishing Company, P.O. Box 32112, El Sereno Station, Los Angeles, Calif. 90032.
A weekly "journal of independent inquiry, concerned with study of the principles which move society on its present course." The word *manas* comes from a common root suggesting "man" or "thinker."

New Dimensions, Foreign Policy Association-Thomas Y. Crowell Company, New York.
A series of booklets suggests how social studies teachers can enrich their teaching, especially about world affairs. Topics already treated: "Simulation Games," "Foreign News and World Views," "Teaching the Comparative Approach to American Studies," "International Education for Spaceship Earth," "Teaching about War and War Prevention."

Social Education, official journal of the National Council for the Social Studies, Washington, D.C. 20036.

UN Publications: *UNESCO Courier, World Health, ILO Panorama;* can be obtained through the Office of Public Information, United Nations, New York, N.Y. 10017.

SELECTED STUDIES

Anthropology Curriculum Project, University of Georgia, Athens.
A program developed for use in the elementary grades dealing with the development of man and his culture, grades 1-7.

Anthropology Curriculum Study Project, Chicago, Ill.
Sponsored by the American Anthropological Association and designed to develop a cross-disciplinary approach to the study of man.

Carnegie-Mellon Project: *Tradition and Change in Four Societies,* Carnegie-Mellon Institute, Pittsburgh, Pa.
A tenth-grade course using an inquiry approach to aid students in gaining some ideas of how race relations in this country are unique and ways in which they are similar to other multiracial societies.

Center for Teaching International Relations, Graduate School of International Studies, University of Denver, Denver, Colo.
The purpose of the center to develop international studies at the secondary level is carried out through these activities: Institutes in Comparative World Politics, the Materials Distribution Center, curriculum development, the *Newsletter,* and other informational services. Topics: conflict resolution, intergroup relations and the workings of power, political development, newspaper analyses, use of evidence in decision making, nationalism, revolution, and intervention.

Center for War/Peace Studies, 218 East 18th Street, New York, N.Y. 10003.
The schools program features in-service education through workshops to assist educators teaching the international dimension of the curriculum. Publishes *Intercom.*

Diablo Valley Education Project, Diablo Valley, Calif.
A "laboratory" of the Center for War/Peace Studies, developing a curriculum guide stressing affective development as basic to educating citizens who can deal constructively with world problems. Suggests six levels of value choices from those involving the promotion and protection of the individual up to those involving a sense of world community.

Human Relations Education Project of Western New York.
A regional cooperative project in the Buffalo-Niagara Falls metropolitan area (forty school districts involved) to improve the teaching of human relations through curriculum development and in-service education activities. Stresses respect for the dignity of every individual and development of more effective personal relationships. Study guides and bibliography for K-12 have been developed.

The Humanities Curriculum Project, Lawrence Stenhouse (project director), British Schools Council and Nuffield Humanities Project, London, England.
Major premises:

1. That controversial issues should be handled in class with the adolescent.
2. That the teacher accepts the need to submit his teaching in controversial issues to the criterion of neutrality, i.e., not promote his own view.

3. That the mode of inquiry in controversial areas should have discussion rather than instruction as its core.
4. That discussion should protect divergence of view rather than consensus.
5. That the teacher as chairman of the discussion should have responsibility for the quality and standards in learning.

Intercultural Understanding Project, Melvin H. Samuels (project director), Allegheny County Board of School Directors, Pittsburgh, Pa., 1971.

Initiated in 1968, a Title III ESEA program designed to develop a more open-minded attitude toward people of other cultures and to develop a more world-minded view. Introductory unit, "The American Teen-Age Subculture," begins the development of basic concepts and skills elaborated in subsequent units. Secondary-level materials are developed for each unit, e.g., "Japan: World Cultures Unit."

UNESCO Associated Schools Project (in education for international cooperation and peace).

Objective: "To develop enlightened and sympathetic attitudes which will be reflected in behaviors and understanding after the pupils have finished school." Aims to promote international understanding through special study programs and experimental activities. Issues a bulletin twice a year, conducts study seminars, and distributes documentation kits including multimedia.

World Law Fund, 11 West 42d Street, New York, N.Y. 10036.

Conducts conferences and seminars; develops curriculum and audiovisual materials; distributes a newsletter.

Index